American Sign Language

A Student Text
Units 19-27

Dennis Cokely
Charlotte Baker-Shenk

Clerc Books
Gallaudet University Press
Washington, D.C.

Clerc Books
An imprint of Gallaudet University Press
Washington, DC 20002

Originally published 1981 by T. J. Publishers, Inc., Silver Spring Maryland
Published 1991 by Gallaudet University Press.
Printed in the United States of America

07 05 03 01   8 7 6 5

Cover design by Auras Design, Washington, DC
Drawings by Frank A. Paul
Photographs by Thomas Klagholz

Photograph of Charlotte Baker-Shenk taken by Viki Kemper.

ISBN 0-930323-88-2

CONTENTS

PREFACE

This text is part of a total, multi-media package designed for the teacher and student of American Sign Language (ASL). Included in this package are two texts for teachers and three texts for students:

American Sign Language: a teacher's resource text on grammar and culture

American Sign Language: a teacher's resource text on curriculum, methods, and evaluation

American Sign Language: a student text (Units 1-9)

American Sign Language: a student text (Units 10-18)

American Sign Language: a student text (Units 19-27)

Also included in this package is a set of five one-hour videotapes which are especially designed to accompany these texts.

As a package, the texts and videotapes provide the teacher with information about the structure of ASL and an interactive approach to teaching the language. They provide the student with carefully prepared ASL dialogues and drills as well as information about the structure of ASL and the Deaf Community.

The videotapes are designed so that there is a one-hour tape for each text. The first tape illustrates all of the examples in the grammar and culture text. The second tape provides a 'live' demonstration of a number of the techniques described in the curriculum, methods, and evaluation text. Each of the final three tapes (one for each student text) not only illustrates the dialogues for a particular text but also provides several ASL stories, poems, and dramatic prose of varying length and difficulty for use in the classroom or language lab.

ACKNOWLEDGEMENTS

It is simply not possible to mention all those individuals whose support and encouragement have made this text possible. Likewise, it would be very difficult to list all those individuals whose own ideas and creativity have influenced this text. However, there are several people we wish to mention by name because of their invaluable assistance in preparing this text:

For their creativity, spontaneity, and hard work in making the videotapes upon which this text is based—Larry Berke, Nathie Couthen, Pat Graybill, Ella Lentz, M.J. Bienvenu, and Gilbert Eastman.

For their patience during long photo sessions and their skill as models of ASL—two native, Deaf Signers: M.J. Bienvenu and Mel Carter, Jr.

For his unique artistic skills, beautiful illustrations, and willingness to keep doing more than what was expected—Frank Allen Paul.

For support, encouragement, and a willingness to "pitch in" and "xerox her brain"—Micky Cokely.

For his "good eye" and many hours spent in producing all of the beautifully clear photographs in this text—Tom Klagholz.

Finally, for typing, re-typing, and more re-typing of various drafts as well as for back rubs, seaweed, greens, and unfailing good cheer during the past three years—Beverly Klayman.

Note To the Teacher:

This text assumes that students are familiar with the information provided in Units 1-18 in this series and possess the ASL skills targeted in those units. This text (Units 19-27) is intended to help your students acquire a higher level of skill in some of the major grammatical features of ASL. Again, each of the nine units focuses on a different grammatical topic in the language. Since this text is part of a three text series, not all aspects of a particular grammatical feature are covered in this text. Rather, these texts form the core of a spiraling curriculum. Thus, the same grammatical topics are covered in each of the three student texts. However, the discussion of each topic becomes more and more complex and detailed as the student progresses on to each higher-level text. There are a total of twenty-seven units (nine units per text) in this series. Each unit focuses on different aspects of the grammar of ASL and the culture of Deaf people.

The format of each unit is described in the section entitled *Note To the Student*. As mentioned in that section, we believe this format allows for a great deal of flexibility. Since you know your own teaching style and how your students learn best, we urge you to use this text in the way you feel is most beneficial. We do recommend that you go through this text at a slower pace than you may be accustomed to. As you look through the text, you will see that there is a lot of information in each unit. Please don't feel that you must go through one unit in each class or each week. We also suggest that you supplement the dialogues and drills with other activities that will reinforce the specific grammatical feature of each unit.

Our aim and hope is that the information provided in each unit will, for the most part, be dealt with by the students on their own time. This will free you to devote more class time toward developing their skills in *using* ASL instead of *talking about* ASL.

The two teacher texts *(Grammar and Culture* and *Curriculum, Methods, and Evaluation)* are an invaluable resource for using these student texts. The *Grammar and Culture* text not only provides a more detailed explanation of each of the grammatical features in the student texts, but it also contains several chapters of vital information that is not covered in these texts. In addition, at the end of each of the grammatical chapters, it contains a more complete transcription of each of the three student-text dialogues which focus on that grammatical topic. The *Curriculum, Methods and Evaluation* text not only explains how to conduct dialogues and drills in the classroom, but also shows you how to develop your own dialogues and drills. In addition, that text contains a large number of activities and exercises which can be used to supplement the dialogues and drills in the student texts.

As you skim through this text one thing should be quite obvious—this is not a vocabulary text. Although there are a large number of *Key Illustrations* and *Supplementary Illustrations,* these do not illustrate every sign that is used in the dialogues. Instead, it is assumed that either your students already know the vocabulary that is not illustrated or that you will provide them with this vocabulary by whatever means you feel is appropriate (use of a reference text, instruction in the classroom, etc.).

One final note: As you may know, variation in a language is the rule rather than the exception. There are always interesting differences in the vocabulary and grammar of different speakers or signers of a language. With this in mind, we have tried to include variations in signs wherever possible so that students will be able to understand a wider variety of ASL Signers. However, due to the limitations of space (and our knowledge), the treatment of sign variation in this text will need your reinforcement and expansion. We ask that you supplement the illustrations found in this text with other variations that you are aware of—especially those used by members of the Deaf Community in your area of the country.

Note To the Student:

Learning a second language is not an easy task. In fact, although learning your first language was probably the easiest thing you've ever done, learning a second language may be among the most difficult things you ever do. Learning a second language (and learning it really well) means learning more than the vocabulary and the grammar of that language. It means learning about the people who use that language—their attitudes, their cultural values, and their way of looking at the world.

Thus, learning American Sign Language as a second language means learning about the group of people who use ASL—the Deaf Community. It means recognizing the Deaf Community as a separate, cultural group with its own set of values, attitudes, and world view. Whatever your personal or professional motivations for wanting to learn ASL, you will find that the more you know about, appreciate, and understand the people who use ASL, the easier it is for you to learn their language.

For most hearing people, learning ASL is quite a different experience than learning a spoken language. First of all, to understand someone who is using ASL, you have to "listen" with your eyes. Most hearing people don't have a lot of experience at this since they have grown up depending mostly on their ears to receive linguistic information. Second, to produce ASL you have to use your eyes, face, hands, and body in ways which are not required by spoken languages. Most hearing people tend to be somewhat inhibited about using their eyes, face, hands, and body for communication. This is especially true for many Americans who have learned that "it is impolite to stare" and who have learned to restrain their body movements in order to be more socially acceptable.

Another important difference is that ASL is not a written language. This means that there are no newspapers, magazines, books, etc., written in ASL. Because ASL does not have a written form, we generally have to use English to write about ASL. This means using English words (called "glosses") when trying to translate the meaning of ASL signs and for trying to write down ASL sentences.

Although this is unavoidable at the present time, it has often led people to the mistaken notions that ASL is "bad English" or "broken English" because the grammar doesn't look like English—yet the "words" (signs) are written with English glosses. A real problem! Unfortunately, using English glosses for ASL signs also often leads students to think that ASL is very much like English, when, in fact, it is very different in many important ways.

Remember, the key to successfully learning any second language is: *accept the language on its own terms with an open mind.* If you have an open mind and an accepting attitude, and if you give yourself time, you will learn ASL. Of course, if you are trying to learn ASL (or any language), the most helpful thing is to communicate as frequently as possible with people who use ASL. While no book can substitute for real, live, human interaction, this text provides you with what we feel is a valuable supplement—carefully developed dialogues which are examples of how Deaf people actually communicate using ASL.

This text (part of a series of three student texts), contains nine units. Each of these units focuses on a topic relating to the grammar of ASL and on some cultural aspect of the Deaf Community. The format for each of these units is as follows:

A. *Synopsis:*	A detailed summary of the dialogue in that Unit.
B. *Cultural Information:*	An explanation of the cultural topic which the dialogue focuses on.
C. *Dialogue:*	A presentation of the dialogue with the two Signers' parts on separate pages.
D. *Key Illustrations:*	Drawings of signs which have been specially prepared for the dialogue so that the face, hands, and body are exactly as they appear in the dialogue. (We have tried to use the best possible angle in all illustrations for presenting both the manual and non-manual aspects of each sign.)
E. *Supplementary Illustration:*	Additional drawings of signs that appear in the dialogue. However, the face or body may be slightly different than the way the signs are used in the dialogue.
F. *General Discussion:*	An explanation of the specific grammatical features of ASL which the dialogue focuses on.
G. *Text Analysis:*	A line-by-line analysis and discussion of parts of the dialogue.
H. *Sample Drills:*	Three drills which provide an opportunity to practice the specific grammatical features described in that Unit.
I. *Video Notes:*	A discussion of some of the important things that are shown in the videotaped version of the dialogue (taken from the videotape designed to accompany this text).

We believe that this format allows you, the student, a great deal of flexibility in using this text. You probably know how you learn best and what you need to help you learn. If you find that this sequence does not best suit your needs, then we encourage you and your teacher to take the sections in the order you find most helpful. For example, you may choose to read the *Dialogue* first and then the *Synopsis* and *Text Analysis*. The point is that you should be actively involved in deciding how to work with the text—and not be controlled by it. Use it in whatever way will best help you learn ASL.

Finally, as you learn ASL, remember that it is the language of a unique cultural group of people. Whenever appropriate, try to improve your skills by interacting with members of that cultural group. Don't be afraid of making mistakes, but learn from your mistakes. And don't overlook your successes; learn from them too. We hope this text will help you not only develop skills in ASL, but also develop an appreciation and respect for the Deaf Community.

Transcription Symbols

In order to understand the dialogues and drills in this text, you will need to read through the following pages very carefully. These pages describe and illustrate the transcription symbols that are used in this text.

You can imagine how difficult it is to "write ASL". To date, there is no standard way of writing ASL sentences. We have tried to develop a transcription system which clearly shows how much information is given in an ASL sentence. Although we have tried to keep this transcription system as simple as possible, it may still seem complex at first. However, with patience and practice, it will become fairly easy to use.

The chart on the following pages lists thirty symbols, with examples and illustrations of how each symbol is used. To read this chart, you should first look at the illustrations of signs and the symbols used to describe them on the left-hand page, and then read through the explanation of each symbol on the right-hand page. The symbols found on these pages describe what the *hands* are doing. (In the parenthesis following the description, we have indicated the first unit in which each symbol appears.) Throughout the text in the *General Discussion* sections, symbols will be introduced which describe what the *eyes, face, head,* and *body* do. The non-manual, grammatical signals which appeared in Units 1-18 are listed at the end of this section.

ILLUSTRATIONS

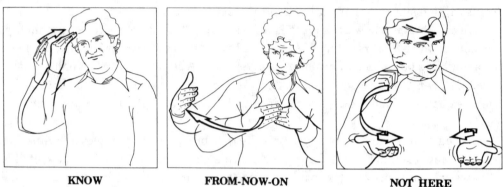

| KNOW | FROM-NOW-ON | NOT HERE |

  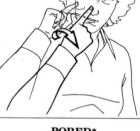

| #WHAT | DIFFERENT+++ | BORED* |

TRANSCRIPTION SYMBOLS

Symbol	Example	Explanation
CAPITAL LETTERS	**KNOW**	An English word in capital letters represents an ASL sign; this word is called a *gloss*. (Unit 1)
-	**FROM-NOW-ON**	When more than one English word is needed to gloss an ASL sign, the English words are separated by a hyphen. (Unit 1)
△	△	A triangle with a letter inside is used to indicate a name sign. (Unit 1)
-	**P-A-T**	When an English word is fingerspelled, the letters in the word are separated by a hyphen. (Unit 2)
‿	**NOT‿HERE**	When two glosses are joined by these curved lines, it indicates that two signs are used in combination. Generally when this happens, there is a change in one or both of the signs so that the combination looks like a single sign. (Unit 1)
#	**#WHAT**	When this symbol is written before a gloss, it indicates the sign is a fingerspelled loan sign. (Unit 1)
+	**DIFFERENT+++**	When a plus sign follows a gloss, this indicates that the sign is repeated. The number of plus signs following the gloss indicates the number of repetitions— e.g. **DIFFERENT+++** indicates the sign is made four times (three repetitions). (Unit 1)
*	**BORED***	An asterisk after a gloss indicates the sign is stressed (emphasized). (Unit 2)

"WHAT" (2h) WHAT'S-UP (2h)alt.GUESS

rt-ASK-TO-*lf* ASSEMBLE-TO-*cntr*

Symbol	Example	Explanation
,	**YESTERDAY, ME**	A comma indicates a grammatical break, signaled by a body shift and/or a change in facial expression (and usually a pause). (Unit 1)
" "	**"WHAT"**	Double quotes around a gloss indicate a gesture. (Unit 1)
(2h)	(2h)**WHAT'S-UP**	This symbol for 'two hands' is written before a gloss and means the sign is made with both hands. (Unit 1)
alt.	(2h)alt.**GUESS**	The symbol 'alt.' means that the hands move in an 'alternating' manner. (Unit 5)
rt *lf* *cntr*	*rt-***ASK-TO-***lf* **ASSEMBLE-TO-***cntr*	The symbol *'rt'* stands for 'right'; *'lf'* for 'left'; and *'cntr'* for 'center'. When a sign is made *in* or *toward* a particular location in space, that place or direction is indicated after the gloss. When a symbol like *'rt'* is written before a gloss, it indicates the location where the sign began. So *rt-***ASK-TO-***lf* indicates that the sign moves from right to left. These symbols refer to the Signer's perspective—e.g. *'rt'* means to the Signer's right. The symbol *'cntr'* is only used when that space directly between the Signer and Addressee represents a particular referent (person, place, or thing). If none of these symbols appear, the sign is produced in neutral space. (Unit 1)

pat-**ASK-TO**-*lee*

me-**CAMERA-RECORD**-*arc*

me-**SHOW**-*arc-lf*

3-CL

L:-CL

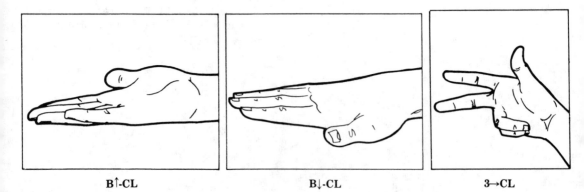

B↑-CL   **B↓-CL**   **3→CL**

Symbol	Example	Explanation
lower case words	*pat*-**ASK-TO**-*lee*	Italicized words that are connected (via hyphens) to the gloss for a verb can also indicate the location where the verb began or ended. For example, if 'Pat' has been given a spatial location on the right, and 'Lee' is on the left, then the sign *pat*-**ASK-TO**-*lee* will move from right to left. These specific words are not used until the things they represent have been given a spatial location. These specific words are used in place of directions like *'rt'* or *'lf'*. (Unit 1)
arc	*me*-**CAMERA-RECORD**-*arc* *me*-**SHOW**-*arc-lf*	When a gloss is followed by the symbol *'arc'*, it means the sign moves in a horizontal arc from one side of the signing space to the other side. If another symbol like *lf* follows the symbol *arc*, it means the arc only includes that part of the signing space. (Unit 3)
-CL	**3-CL**	This symbol for *classifier* is written after the symbol for the handshape that is used in that classifier. (Unit 5)
:	**L:-CL**	This symbol indicates that the handshape is 'bent'—as in a 'bent-**L**' handshape where the index finger is crooked, rather than straight. (Unit 5)
↑	**B↑-CL**	An arrow pointing upward indicates that the palm is facing upward. (Unit 6)
↓	**B↓-CL**	An arrow pointing downward indicates that the palm is facing downward. (Unit 5)
→	**3→CL**	An arrow pointing to the right indicates that the fingers are not facing upwards. This is used to distinguish two sets of classifiers: **3-CL** and **3→CL**; **1-CL** and **1→CL**. (Unit 5)

^{1}outline-CL'circular table'

1-CL'person come up
to me from rt'

5:↓-CL@*rt*

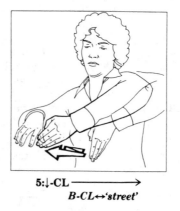

5:↓-CL ⟶
B-CL↔'street'

Symbol	Example	Explanation
outline	1_{outline}-CL'circular table'	This symbol indicates that the hand-shape is used to 'outline' a particular shape. (Unit 5)
' '	1-CL'person come up to me'	Single quotes around a lower case word or words is used to help describe the meaning of a classifier in the context of that sentence. (Unit 5)
@	5:↓-CL@*rt*	This symbol indicates a particular type of movement that is often used when giving something a spatial location. It is characterized by a certain tenseness and a 'hold' at the end of the movement. In this example, the classifier for a large mass is given a spatial location to the Signer's right. (Unit 5)
CAPITAL LETTERS	**RESTAURANT** *INDEX-lf*	When a sign is made with the non-dominant hand, it is written in italics. When an italicized gloss is written under another gloss, it means both hands make separate signs at the same time. In this example, the dominant hand makes the sign **RESTAURANT** while the non-dominant hand points to the left. (Unit 1)
⟶	5:↓-CL ⟶ *B-CL*↔'*street*'	An arrow proceeding from a gloss means that the handshape of that sign is held in its location during the time period shown by the arrow. In this example, the dominant hand 'holds' the 5:↓ classifier in its location while the non-dominant hand indicates a 'street' with the 'B' hand-shape classifier. The symbol ↔ means that the 'B' handshape moves back and forth. (Unit 3)

WAIT*"long time"*

DISCUSS-WITH
"each other" +*"regularly"*

$\overline{\quad\quad\quad q}$
RIGHT

Symbol	Example	Explanation
" "	"open window"	Double quotes around a word or words in lower case indicate a mimed action. (Unit 9)
" "	**WAIT***"long time"*	Double quotes around an italicized word or words in lower case after a gloss indicates that a specific movement is added to that sign. The word or words inside the quotes is the name for that specific movement. (Unit 8)
" "+" "	**DISCUSS-WITH** *"each other"+"regularly"*	When a plus sign joins two or more specific movements, it means those movements occur simultaneously with that sign. (Unit 8)
————	$\overline{}^{q}$ **RIGHT**	A line on top of a gloss or glosses means that a certain non-manual (eyes, face, head, body) signal occurs during the time period shown by the line. At the end of the line, there is a letter(s) which indicates what the non-manual signal is. For example, 'q' represents the signal for a 'yes-no' question. (Unit 1)
( )	(gaze lf) △-*lf*	Words in parentheses on top of a gloss or glosses are used to indicate other movements of the eyes, head, and body. (The word 'gaze' refers to where the Signer looks.) (Unit 1)

SYMBOL	ILLUSTRATIONS

q *('yes-no question')*

    (These photos also illustrate what is meant by a 'brow raise', often written as *'br raise'* or simply, *'br'*.)

$$\overline{\text{q}}$$
YOU

$$\overline{\text{q}}$$
YOU

wh-q *('wh-word question')*

    (These photos also illustrate what is meant by a 'brow squint', often written as *'br squint'*.)

$$\overline{\text{wh-q}}$$
WHO

$$\overline{\text{wh-q}}$$
WHICH

$$\overline{\text{wh-q}}$$
WHERE

rhet.q (*'rhetorical question'*)

$$\frac{\text{rhet.q}}{\text{WHO}}$$

$$\frac{\text{rhet.q}}{\text{WHY}}$$

$$\frac{\text{rhet.q}}{\text{HOW}}$$

t *('topic')*

$$\overline{\text{MORNING}}^{\,t} \qquad \overline{\text{PAPER}}^{\,t}$$

Notice the difference between the *'t'* signal and the *'q'* signal in the two photos on the right.

$$\overline{\text{PAPER}}^{\,t} \qquad \overline{\text{PAPER}}^{\,q}$$

cond *('conditional')*

Conditionals have two parts. The first part is indicated with *'cond'*. The sequence on the right illustrates the conditional sentence 'If it rains, I'll go'.

$$\overline{\text{RAIN}}^{\,cond} \qquad\qquad\qquad \text{GO-}lf$$

neg *('negation')*

    (Signal includes head-
    shaking, not visible in
    photographs)

$$\overline{\text{neg}}$$
NOT

$$\overline{\text{neg}}$$
ME

$$\overline{\text{neg}}$$
FEEL

$$\overline{\text{neg}}$$
FEEL

nod+ tight lips *('assertion')*

    (The 'nod' is more visible
    in drawings in the text.)

$$\overline{\text{nod+ tight lips}}$$
TRUE

AN INTRODUCTION TO PIDGIN SIGN ENGLISH

In order to understand and appreciate the role of American Sign Language in the Deaf Community, students need to remember that there is another language which members of the Community also use. This second language is the language of the hearing majority in the United States—namely, English. In general, interaction between members of the Community occurs in ASL and interaction with non-members of the Community occurs in spoken or written English or in some form of English-influenced signing. Thus, members of the Deaf Community exist in a *bilingual situation*. In addition, sometimes a third language is involved when members of the Deaf Community have strong ethnic ties—for example, to a Spanish-speaking community. Thus, some members of the Deaf Community may exist in a *tri-lingual situation*.

Inside the Deaf Community, ASL plays a very important role. First of all, it enables effective and intimate person-to-person communication. Second, when Deaf people use ASL, they are showing their support for the values and goals of the Community. And that use of ASL helps to identify the people who are members of the Deaf Community.

However, the vast majority of parents, teachers, doctors, psychologists, speech therapists, audiologists, religious workers, and employers that contact and work with Deaf people are hearing speakers of English who do not know ASL. So how do these two groups of people communicate with each other? Most often they interact with each other through the use of Pidgin Sign English—a type of signing which combines certain features of both ASL and English.

A *pidgin* is a means of communication which develops naturally when people who do not know each other's language want to or have to communicate with each other. For example, in Hawaii, various groups of people with different native languages (e.g. English, Chinese, Japanese) use Hawaiian Pidgin English as one way of communicating with each other. Certain tribes in Venezuela use Pidgin Spanish when they interact with traders in the area. In Ireland, tinkers are reported to use an Anglo-Irish Pidgin. Pidgin French is spoken on the Ivory Coast and in other former French possessions on the West African coast. Cameroons Pidgin English is used by over one million speakers in the Cameroons and in Eastern Nigeria. Some other known pidgins are: Australian Pidgin English, New Caladonia Pidgin French, Pidgin Eskimo, Pidgin Dutch, Pidgin Arabic, Asmara Pidgin Italian, China Coast Pidgin English, Korean Pidgin English, New Guinea Pidgin English, and Solomon Islands Pidgin English.

These examples help to illustrate the fact that pidgins are used all over the world. In fact, it has been estimated that 2-3 million people use some form of pidgin every day in at least some language situations. The development and use of pidgins can be

1

seen as a natural human response to a situation in which groups of people want to communicate with each other but do not share the same native language. Normally, a pidgin is no one's native language—that is, children do not grow up using a pidgin as their first language. Rather, pidgins are generally used solely for contact with members of the other language community.

Pidgin Sign English (PSE) has traditionally been one of the major ways in which members of the Deaf Community have interacted with people (mostly hearing) who are not members of the Community. Like all pidgins, PSE is formed by combining certain vocabulary items and grammatical features of the native languages of the two groups. In the case of PSE, these two languages are American Sign Language and English.

Like all pidgins, there is not a single set of fixed rules which can be used to describe PSE. Rather, there are many forms of PSE which differ depending on whether a person uses more of the grammatical structures of ASL or more of the grammatical structures of English.

The varieties of PSE used by Deaf people tend to include more of the grammatical features found in ASL and less of the grammatical structures of English. On the other hand, the varieties of PSE used by hearing people tend to include more of the grammatical features of English and less of the grammatical structures of ASL. As a person's signing moves from English-like signing to ASL, there are different stages which are less and less like English and more and more like ASL. The opposite is true as a person's signing moves from ASL to English-like signing. Thus, there is a continuum of varieties of PSE—some more like English, some more like ASL. The following diagram illustrates this continuum.

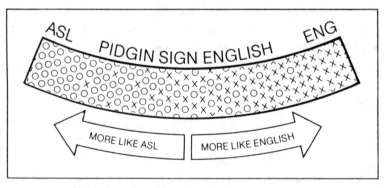

Variation along the ASL-English continuum

In this diagram, the symbol 'o' represents features of ASL and the symbol 'x' represents features of English. Notice that in the middle there is a mixture of both symbols. However, moving toward ASL, there are fewer and fewer 'x's—which indicates that fewer and fewer features of English are present. Likewise, as one moves from ASL to English-like signing, there are fewer and fewer 'o's—which indicates that fewer and fewer features of ASL are present.

This diagram illustrates what has been called a *bilingual continuum*. This continuum is a way of describing the interaction of two languages (ASL and English) that are in contact with each other. One result of this contact has been the natural evolution of a pidgin which can have a variety of forms depending upon how much ASL or English individuals know, or how much ASL or English they use in a given situation.

Although there are many different forms of PSE, there are also two general characteristics which they have in common:

(a) The meaning of each sign is usually the same as its meaning in ASL. In other words, the vocabulary which is used tends to follow the semantics of ASL. Thus, PSE is unlike various manual codes for English which use signs as if they had the same meaning as the English words commonly used to gloss those signs.

(b) The order of signs tends to follow the word order of English.

Some varieties of more English-like PSE also use signs for the English copula (e.g. 'is', 'are', 'be') and the English articles 'a' and 'the'. However, other varieties of more English-like PSE do not use these signs. More ASL-like varieties of PSE use, to differing degrees, various grammatical features of ASL such as verb directionality, number incorporation, and non-manual signals.

It is important to remember why people use PSE (or pidgins in general)—that is, to make it possible for them to *communicate* with each other when they don't know each other's language. Thus, the people involved in the conversation and their respective ASL and English skills are important factors in determining which variety of PSE will be used, whether it be more like ASL or more like English.

Some of the variation which exists in PSE is illustrated in the following example:

Suppose the Signer wants to tell another person that Pat gave the boxes to the teacher yesterday. If the Signer wants to convey this message in ASL, s/he may sign:

> _____ (gaze rt _____) t (gaze lf _____)
> **ONE-DAY-PAST   P-A-T-*rt*   BOX+ -*rt*,   *pat*-GIVE-TO-*lf*   TEACH⁀AGENT-*lf***

or

> ____t____   (gaze rt)   (gaze lf _____)
> **BOX+,   ONE-DAY-PAST   P-A-T-*rt*   *pat*-GIVE-TO-*lf*   TEACH⁀AGENT-*lf***

However, suppose the Signer does not have much skill in ASL but knows some signs and wants to express the same meaning. S/he might sign:

> **P-A-T   *me*-GIVE-TO-*you*   BOX+   TO   TEACH   AGENT   ONE-DAY-PAST**

Notice that the Signer used repetition of the sign **BOX** to show plurality. However, the Signer has not used any of the non-manual signals which occur in ASL—like eye gaze or the signal for topics. The Signer did not assign a location to 'Pat' or the 'teacher'. Thus, the verb ____-GIVE-TO-____ does not correctly 'agree with' its subject and object. In fact, the movement of the verb (from the Signer toward the Addressee) makes it look like the Signer is the subject and the Addressee is the object. The Signer also did not sign **TEACH AGENT** as 'joined' signs (as they would occur in ASL). Finally, the Signer basically followed English word order ('Pat gave the books to the teacher yesterday'). Clearly, this is an example of a more English-like variety of ASL.

Now suppose the Signer has more skill in ASL (knows more of the grammatical features of ASL) and wants to express the same meaning. S/he might sign:

(gaze rt)   (gaze lf   )   (gaze lf)
 P-A-T-*rt*   *pat*-**GIVE-TO**-*lf*   **BOX+**   **INDEX**-*lf*   **TEACH AGENT**-*lf*   **ONE-DAY-PAST**

Notice that the Signer still has followed English word order, but has used several other features of ASL. 'Pat' was given a location in space by fingerspelling the name to the right and gazing to the right. The verb ____-**GIVE-TO**-____ moved from right to left and, thus, 'agreed with' its subject, 'Pat', and object, 'teacher'. The sign **BOX** has been repeated to show plurality, and **TEACH AGENT** was signed like a single, joined sign rather than two separate signs as in the first PSE example. The object 'teacher' was also clearly given a location in space by pointing and gazing to the left before signing the noun in that location. This is an example of a more ASL-like variety of PSE.

As you can see, there are many ways in which a person's signing can vary depending on how much ASL or English s/he knows. Again, it is important to remember that the primary reason why people use PSE is that they aren't sufficiently competent or comfortable in the other person's language to express themselves in that language. Of course, not all Deaf people and Hearing people will be able to communicate with each other—even in PSE. For example, if the Hearing person doesn't know much ASL and the Deaf person doesn't know much English, they may not be able to use a variety of PSE which is mutually understandable. So using PSE does not guarantee successful communication.

However, PSE has become an accepted means of interaction between Deaf and Hearing people. It is not difficult to understand why this is so. First, until rather recently, ASL was not accepted as a valid, fully-formed language by Hearing people. ASL was often viewed as "bad language" or "broken English". Second, until rather recently, Hearing people did not learn ASL in "sign language" classes. Instead, they learned lists of signs but used these signs according to the grammatical structure of English. Third, because of prevailing educational attitudes (remember that about 90% of the educators in the field of Deaf education are Hearing people), Deaf people have been taught that anything that approaches English (like PSE) is valued and anything that is not English (ASL) is "bad language" and, thus, is not valued. Fourth, the Deaf Community has been understandably reluctant to share its language with Hearing people for fear that Hearing people will use it to exert influence in the Community and gain even more power over Deaf people.

Whereas members of the Deaf Community generally view PSE as a more "safe" and acceptable means of communication with Hearing people, they generally hold a very different view of artificially developed manual codes for English (MCE) like Signing Exact English (SEE II), Seeing Essential English (SEE I), and Signed English (a system developed for use with very young deaf children). Most members of the Deaf Community view these codes as an "intrusion" on ASL, an attempt to change their language in unnatural ways. Thus, their response to the use of these invented codes has generally been quite negative.

Consider how speakers of English would react if someone (a non-native, non-fluent speaker of English) tried to force them to use the word 'tsork' to refer to a black or green piece of slate used in schools to write on. There are at least two reasons why people would resist using this 'word': first, no native English word begins with the sounds [ts] and second, English speakers already have a way of referring to the writing surface described above—'blackboard'.

Sometimes, people with a limited knowledge of ASL will either invent signs or try to change the meanings of ASL signs. These people (primarily educators) generally feel that signs should represent English words. Since ASL signs do *not* represent English words, it is easy to understand why the Deaf Community often reacts quite negatively to such unnatural attempts to change ASL. For example, suppose someone wanted to express the following meanings: 'go fast by foot', 'compete', 'a rip or tear', and 'liquid flowing'. In many languages, there are separate words or signs for each of these meanings.

ASL:	GO-FAST-BY-FOOT	COMPETE
French:	'courir'	'couler'
German:	'laufen'	'fliessen'

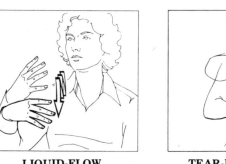

ASL:	LIQUID-FLOW	TEAR-IN-STOCKING
French:	'échelle'	'poser sa candidature'
German:	'Laufmasche'	'kandibieren'

However, there are many people who do not know or will not accept the fact that ASL has separate signs for these meanings. These people, knowingly or unknowingly, feel that Signers should just use a single sign **(GO-FAST-BY-FOOT)** to convey these four meanings because English uses a single word ('run') for all four meanings. They think it is allright to change ASL like this because they think it will help Deaf people learn English (so far, an unproven assumption). Naturally, Deaf people angrily resist this kind of oppression of their language.

However, whereas members of the Deaf Community generally resist using these codes and interacting with people who use them, they are much more accepting of PSE and people who use PSE. This is because the primary purpose of PSE is *communication* (not the teaching of English by changing ASL) and because PSE Signers generally use signs according to the meanings they have in ASL.

In summary, PSE is not an unchanging, easily identifiable point on the continuum. It is a blending of features of ASL and English which can have many different forms. It is not a system of manually coding English as are SEE I, SEE II, etc. It was not artificially developed for the purpose of representing English; rather, it evolved naturally from the bilingual situation in which users of ASL and users of English interact with each other. The "rules" of PSE are variable, depending upon the Signer's skills, the situation, the topic, etc. The primary goal of people who use PSE is successful communication, not an exact representation of English. Because of this focus on meaning and communication, PSE has been a relatively comfortable way for users of ASL and users of English to interact—although the degree of mutual comfort depends on how much the interactants know each other's base language.

Unit 19

Sentence Types

A. Synopsis

Pat and Lee are having lunch at a restaurant. Pat checks to see if Lee was at Gallaudet College in 1973. Lee says that s/he was a junior and asks why Pat wants to know. Pat has heard that the statue of Gallaudet is missing. Lee says that actually the government has borrowed it—maybe to replace it. Pat can't believe all the changes that have happened at Gallaudet. Lee imagines that if someone who graduated in 1950 came to visit, they'd be really shocked. Pat agrees and remarks that his/her mother—a 1959 graduate—was stunned when she visited last year. Lee says that if the two of them go to visit in 15 years, they would see that things have changed again.

B. Cultural Information: Gallaudet College

In 1856, a man named Amos Kendall donated some land in the northeast part of Washington, D.C. to establish a school for Deaf and Blind children. This school was incorporated in 1857 as The Columbia Institution for the Deaf and Dumb and Blind, and Edward Miner Gallaudet (the son of Thomas Hopkins Gallaudet) became its first superintendent. During the next several years, E. M. Gallaudet worked to establish a college division at the school. In April of 1864, the U.S. Congress passed a law, signed by President Abraham Lincoln, which established The National Deaf Mute College as part of the Columbia Institution. Congress then increased its support of the College over the following years and provided funds to purchase additional land, erect new buildings, and establish free scholarships. During this time, the Blind students were transferred from Kendall School to the Maryland School for the Blind.

In 1869, the first College class graduated—all males. Females were not permitted to enter the College until 1887. In 1891, a "Normal Department" was established to train hearing teachers. In 1894, the name of the College was changed to Gallaudet College in honor of Thomas Hopkins Gallaudet. Edward Miner Gallaudet served as President of the College until 1910 when he retired. Other important dates in the history of Gallaudet College are:

1937—a Research Department was established
1957—Gallaudet College became accredited
1969—the Model Secondary School for the Deaf (MSSD) was established
1970—the Kendall Demonstration Elementary School (KDES) was established

Gallaudet College, the world's only accredited liberal arts college for Deaf students, has an average enrollment of 1500 students from all over the United States,

Canada, and several foreign countries. MSSD has approximately 350 students, and KDES has approximately 160 students. Several years ago, the college instituted a Ph.D. program in Administration, cooperated in establishing the National Center for Law and the Deaf on its campus, established a Center for Continuing Education, and now is continuing to increase the number of its graduate programs. More information on Gallaudet College can be obtained by writing: Office of Alumni & Public Relations, Gallaudet College, Kendall Green, Washington, D.C. 20002.

C. Dialogue

Pat

Pat₁:
```
            co                 (gaze at signing hand          )              q
      "HEY", YOU PAST+ GALLAUDET NINETEEN SEVEN THREE, RIGHT YOU
```

Pat₂:
```
      _____q  nod  (gaze rt        )
      KNOW+ YOU STATUE GALLAUDET,       SOMEONE-rt  rt-TELL-me  MISSING
```

Pat₃:
```
      _____wh-q
      BORROW-FROM-rt  FOR-FOR
```

Pat₄:
```
              _____t                       _____neg
      "HEY" GALLAUDET INDEX-rt, MANY* CHANGE+, "WOW"+, CAN'T BELIEVE
```

Pat₅:
```
      nodding           _____nod                        _____nod
            SAME-AS MY MOTHER, GRADUATE NINETEEN FIVE NINE INDEX-rt,

      _____cs          (gaze rt)
      ONE-YEAR-PASTwg GO-TO-rt VISIT, SHOCK*
```

Pat₆: "THAT'S-RIGHT" TRUE

Lee

Lee₁:
<pre>
     nodding (gaze lf, 'thinking'   )   neg   nod   wh-q
              ME SOPHOMORE   "NO-NO", JUNIOR RIGHT+,   WHYwg
</pre>

Lee₂:
<pre>
                                neg
     "HOLD-IT", MISSING NOT, GOVERNMENT BORROW-FROM-lf
</pre>

Lee₃:
<pre>
                                               neg
     (2h)"WELL" (2h)NOT-KNOW, SEEM REPLACE, (2h)NOT-KNOW+
</pre>

Lee₄:
<pre>
     nodding   (gaze rt)   cond
     TRUE+, SUPPOSE   DEAF INDEX-rt,

     AGE++ GRADUATE GALLAUDET NINETEEN FIFTY THEREABOUTS,

                                    (gaze lf)
     FROM-rt-GO-TO-lf VISIT, INDEX-rt   STUNNED* "WHEW"
</pre>

Lee₅:
<pre>
                                                                     cond
     "PSHAW", SUPPOSE FIFTEEN YEAR FUTURE US-TWO GO-TO-lf VISIT,

     (gaze lf)
            GALLAUDET AGAIN CHANGE
</pre>

Lee₆: "PSHAW"

Note: Some people use the gloss **MIND⌒FROZEN** for the sign that we gloss as **STUNNED** in Lee₅.

D. Key Illustrations

Pat

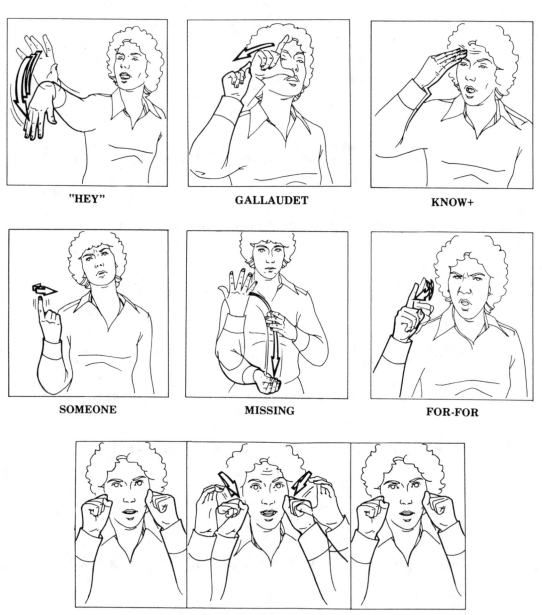

"HEY"   GALLAUDET   KNOW+

SOMEONE   MISSING   FOR-FOR

SHOCK*

Lee

SOPHOMORE

JUNIOR

NOT

REPLACE

STUNNED*

US-TWO

E. Supplementary Illustrations

lf-TELL-*me*

BORROW-FROM-*lf*

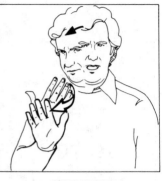

NOT-KNOW

SEEM+

CHANGE

THINK SAME-AS

F. General Discussion: Sentence Types

The previous discussions of sentence types in ASL (Units 1 and 10) have dealt with 'yes-no' questions, 'wh-word' questions, commands, topics, negation, rhetorical questions, and conditionals. This section will briefly review the information presented so far and will present additional information about some of these areas. In addition, this section will briefly describe relative clauses in ASL. At this point, it is assumed that the reader can comfortably and accurately comprehend and produce the range of sentence types and grammatical signals which occurred in Units 1-18.

Questions in ASL:

There are three basic types of questions in ASL—'yes-no' questions, 'wh-word' questions, and rhetorical questions. Each of these question types has its own set of non-manual behaviors which can be seen in the photos below.

q
YOU

wh-q
WHO

rhet.q
WHO

'Yes-no' questions are questions which, in principle, can be answered by giving a simple "yes" or "no" response. For example, it is possible to respond to a 'yes-no' question by using a single sign (e.g. **YES, NO, MAYBE**) or a headnod, headshake, or shoulder-shrug. The non-manual signal '*q*' which occurs with the sentence shows that it is a 'yes-no' question.

On the other hand, 'wh-word' questions cannot be answered by responding "yes" or "no". Instead, these questions require a response that provides additional information about something. The type of response depends on the 'wh-word' sign which occurs in the question—e.g. **WHO, WHERE, WHY, WHAT'S-UP, FOR-FOR, #DO-DO, "WHAT", HOW, #WHAT.** This sign often occurs at the end of the question although it may also occur at the beginning—or may itself serve as the question.

Rhetorical questions are not true questions since the Addressee is not expected to respond. Rather, a rhetorical question is a way for the Signer to introduce and draw attention to certain information that s/he will then supply. In effect, the Signer asks a question and then responds to it him/herself. In general, rhetorical questions involve the use of a 'wh-word' sign such as **WHY, "WHAT", WHO,** or **HOW.** Rhetorical questions may also be asked using the sign **REASON** (which then has a meaning very similar to the sign **WHY**).

Commands in ASL:

Commands are sentences that order the Addressee to do something. In general, commands are indicated by stress (emphasis) on the verb and usually involve direct eye gaze at the Addressee. This stress (*) usually involves making the sign faster and sharper than normal.

There is another form of stress that is used when the Signer wants to be very emphatic. This form of stress involves a slower and very deliberate movement while looking very sharply at the Addressee. This type of slow, deliberate movement is stronger (more emphatic) than the fast, sharp stress. For example, it might be used when the Signer anticipates that the Addressee will not want to obey the command; so the Signer issues the command very emphatically.

Conditionals in ASL:

A conditional sentence has two parts: a part that states a condition and a part that states what will happen if that condition is or is not met (i.e. the result). In ASL, the condition portion is generally signed first and is accompanied by the non-manual behaviors seen in the photo below.

<u>cond</u>
RAIN

Notice that the non-manual behaviors include a brow raise, usually with the head tilted in one direction, and, sometimes, the body slightly inclined in that direction. These non-manual behaviors are held for the duration of the condition segment of the sentence. After the condition, there is a slight break (pause) and the non-manual behaviors change to those that are appropriate for the result segment (e.g. command, question).

Although the condition segment may be introduced by using a sign such as **SUPPOSE, IF,** or **#IF,** often the only indication that a sentence is a conditional is the non-manual signal described above. (See the *General Discussion* in Unit 10 for additional review, and notice in the example how the change in non-manual behaviors during the result segment depends on whether the result is a statement or a question.)

Negation and Assertion in ASL:

Signs or sentences can be negated by using the non-manual *'neg'* signal, or by using a negation sign like **NOT, CAN'T, NONE,** and **NEVER,** or by using both the *'neg'* signal and a negation sign together. The non-manual behaviors in the *'neg'* signal include a side-to-side headshake, frequently accompanied by a frown, and sometimes a brow squint, a wrinkling of the nose, and/or a raised upper lip. This signal basically means 'not' and is seen in the photos below (except the headshake is not visible).

neg
FEEL

neg
NOT

When a negation signs does occur in a sentence, it (and often the whole sentence) is usually accompanied by the 'neg' signal. The negation sign often occurs before the verb. However, it sometimes occurs at the end of the sentence. When the negation sign occurs at the end of the sentence, it seems that the Signer is emphasizing the negation. This is frequently seen in dramatic or artistic performances in ASL. In addition, some Signers may emphasize the negation by using the sign twice in the sentence—often before the verb and at the end of the sentence (where it is often stressed).

Just as the English word 'not' is frequently used in contractions like 'isn't', 'can't', and 'won't', there are some negation signs which often occur in "joined signs". Some examples of this are shown below.

NOT⌣HERE   WHY⌣NOT   NOT⌣POLITE

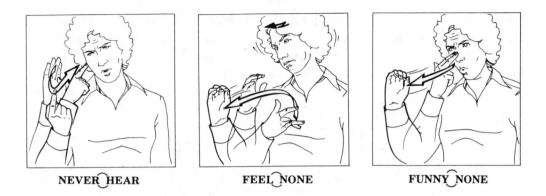

NEVER⌣HEAR   FEEL⌣NONE   FUNNY⌣NONE

Returning to the *'neg'* signal, recall then one usual component of this signal is a brow *squint*. But suppose the sentence is a 'yes-no' question like 'Don't you remember that?'. One component of the *'q'* signal is a brow *raise*. So what will happen when both the *'neg'* and *'q'* signals occur in a sentence? The two photographs below illustrate the result. Compare these with the previous illustrations of the *'q'* signal alone and the *'neg'* signal alone.

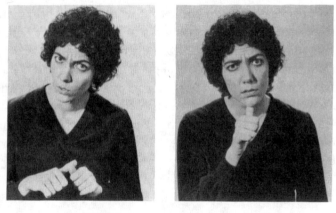

neg+ q   neg+ q
REMEMBER   NOT

Assertions in ASL are usually signaled by a headnod *('nod')* or repeated headnodding *('nodding')* —which emphasizes that something 'is true', 'did happen', 'will happen', etc. Often, this nod or nodding is accompanied by a tightening of the closed lips *('tight lips'),* as shown below with the sign **WILL.**

nod	nodding
WILL	**ENJOY**

Topic-Comment Structure in ASL:

In general, ASL can be classified as a *topic-comment* language. This means that ASL Signers tend to indicate first the thing they want to talk about (called the *topic*) and then make some statement(s), question(s), etc., about that thing (called the *comment*). To show which elements constitute the topic, Signers use the non-manual *'t'* signal—which accompanies all of the signs in the topic. The behaviors in this signal are a brow raise, head tilt, and fairly constant eye gaze on the Addressee. The last sign in the topic is also held slightly longer than usual, resulting in a "pause". Then, when the *comment* is signed, the head position, brows, and gaze direction change. How they change depends on the type of comment that follows (e.g. statement, 'yes-no' question, command). The two photographs below illustrate the non-manual behaviors in the *'t'* signal. (Notice the variation in handshape with the sign **PAPER.**)

t	t
PAPER	**PAPER**

Sometimes the *topic* portion of a sentence is introduced by one of the following signs: **KNOW-THAT, YOU KNOW,** or **KNOW.** In general, the signs **KNOW-THAT** or **YOU KNOW** are used when the Signer thinks the Addressee is familiar with the topic. These signs are used to draw attention to the familiar topic. If the Signer is not sure if the Addressee is familiar with the topic, s/he may use the sign **KNOW** (which may have repeated movement). Generally, the Signer will then pause slightly longer between the topic and comment while waiting for some indication that the Addressee is indeed familiar with the topic. If the Addressee responds positively, the Signer will continue with the comment. If the response is negative, the Signer will provide further clarification or explanation of the topic and then continue with the comment. In effect, the Signer is using the topic to function as a 'yes-no' question in order to make sure the Addressee is familiar with the topic—e.g. 'You know Pat? (Addressee responds positively by nodding) Yeah, well yesterday . . .'

| KNOW-THAT | YOU KNOW | KNOW |

Relative Clauses in ASL:

One final type of sentence is a sentence which has a *restrictive relative clause* in it. Relative clauses help identify the specific person or thing that the Signer wants to talk about. For example, in the English sentence, 'The woman *who just kissed me* is my wife', the words in italics form a restrictive relative clause that helps identify *which* woman is the speaker's wife.

In ASL, there is a non-manual signal (that we write as *'rel.cl'*) that occurs with all of the signs in the relative clause. This signal includes a brow raise, backward tilt of the head, and often a cheek and upper lip raise. There is no pause between the relative clause and the rest of the sentence. An example of a sentence with a restrictive relative clause is seen below.

Context   The Signer is walking with a girlfriend and notices another good friend across the street on the right. The Signer tells her companion:

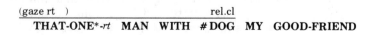

THAT-ONE*-*rt*   MAN   WITH   #DOG   MY   GOOD-FRIEND

'That guy (who is) with the dog is a good friend of mine.'

Sentences with restrictive relative clauses do not seem to occur as frequently in ASL as the other types of sentences.

This discussion has summarized much of the information presented in Units 1 and 10 and has provided an introduction to relative clauses in ASL. The *Text Analysis* sections throughout Units 1-27 also provide additional information and examples of the various sentence types in ASL and the non-manual signals which help distinguish them.

G. Text Analysis

```
                 co                      (gaze at signing hand        )  _____q
Pat₁:    "HEY",  YOU  PAST+  GALLAUDET  NINETEEN  SEVEN  THREE,  RIGHT  YOU
```

```
                 (gaze at signing hand           )
      •  NINETEEN  SEVEN  THREE,
```
> Notice that the Signer gazes at the signing hand. Signers frequently do this when they are unsure of an exact date or when they are fingerspelling a word and are not sure of the exact spelling.

```
                        q
      •  RIGHT   YOU
```
> Notice that this is a 'yes-no' question. The Signer wants to know if the previous information is correct. The non-manual signal for this type of question is illustrated in the *General Discussion* section.

```
         nodding (gaze lf, 'thinking'    )  ___neg___  ___nod___   _____wh-q
Lee₁:             ME  SOPHOMORE  "NO-NO",  JUNIOR  RIGHT+,  WHYwg
```

```
      •  nodding
         _____
```
> Notice that Lee responds to Pat's question by nodding (meaning 'that is true') and then supplies additional information.

```
         (gaze lf,  'thinking'        )
      •     ME   SOPHOMORE
```
> The sign **SOPHOMORE** (see illustration above) involves contact with the middle finger of the non-dominant hand. The sign **JUNIOR** (see illustration above) involves contact with the index finger of the non-dominant hand. Other signs for collegiate and high school academic standing involve similar contact: **SENIOR** (contact with non-dominant thumb), **FRESHMAN** (contact with non-dominant ring finger), **PREP** (contact with non-dominant little finger).

          <u>   neg   </u>
- **"NO-NO"**

> This gesture (waving both hands back and forth) and the accompanying negative non-manual behaviors are used to indicate that the previous information is not correct.

          <u>   nod   </u>
- **JUNIOR**

> Notice that the sign **JUNIOR** is accompanied by a head nod. This indicates that the information is true (in contrast to the previous information). See the section on assertions in the *General Discussion*.

         <u>   wh-q   </u>
- **WHYwg**

> Notice that the Signer uses a variant of the sign **WHY** with the appropriate non-manual signal for this type of question. Compare the following illustrations of the sign **WHY** and two variants of the sign. Notice how repeating the movement in the variants is one way of "holding the sign longer"—which is frequently done at the end of a question.

<u>wh-q</u>	<u>wh-q</u>	<u>wh-q</u>
WHY	**WHYwg**	**WHYwg**

                                <u>q</u> <u>nod</u> (gaze rt   )

Pat₂: <u>**KNOW+ YOU STATUE GALLAUDET,**</u>   **SOMEONE-*rt* *rt*-TELL-*me* MISSING**

                                                  <u>q</u>
- **KNOW+ YOU STATUE GALLAUDET**

> Notice that Pat uses this question to introduce a new topic to the conversation. In this case Lee responds affirmatively to the question and Pat makes a comment about the statue. If Lee had responded negatively, Pat would probably have supplied further information—a description of the statue, its location, etc.—which would have helped Lee remember the statue.

<u>nod</u> (gaze rt   )
- **SOMEONE-*rt* *rt*-TELL-*me***

> Notice that Lee must have responded affirmatively to Pat's initial question because Pat 'nods' and continues on with the comment. This is similar to what happens in English when a person says "Do you remember Bev? Good. Well, yesterday . . .".
>
> Notice also that the directional verb *rt*-**TELL**-*me* 'agrees with' its subject—**SOMEONE**-*rt*. Further information on verbs of this type can be found in Units 4, 13, and 22.

                                        neg

Lee₂: "HOLD-IT", MISSING NOT, GOVERNMENT BORROW-FROM-*lf*

                                      neg
- **MISSING NOT,**

> Notice that the negation sign **NOT** occurs after the sign **MISSING**. When negation signs occur at the end of a sentence, it seems to make the negation more emphatic. Notice also that the non-manual signal for negation occurs with the sign **NOT**. The behaviors in this signal are described in the *General Discussion* section.

- **BORROW-FROM-*lf***

> This sign serves to establish Gallaudet College to Lee's left. Notice how this location (Lee's left, Pat's right) is maintained for all future references to Gallaudet College.

                                    wh-q
<u>   </u>

Pat₃: **BORROW-FROM-*rt* FOR-FOR**

> This is an example of a 'wh-word' question in ASL. As such, the non-manual signal for 'wh-word' questions occurs throughout the question. The *General Discussion* sections of Units 1, 10, and 19 provide a description of the behaviors in this signal.

                                t   neg

Pat₄: "HEY" GALLAUDET INDEX-*rt*, MANY* CHANGE+, "WOW"+, CAN'T BELIEVE

                                      t
- **GALLAUDET INDEX-*rt***

> Notice that Pat maintains the location established earlier for Gallaudet College (Lee₂).

- **MANY* CHANGE+**

> The sign **MANY** has been stressed to emphasize the fact that there have been a large number of changes. Notice also that the sign **CHANGE** is repeated. This also reinforces the fact that more than one change has occurred.

	nodding	(gaze rt)	cond
Lee$_4$:   TRUE+,   SUPPOSE   DEAF   INDEX-*rt*,

               nodding
- **TRUE+,**

    Notice the nodding that occurs with this sign. This use of nodding with the sign **TRUE** is described in the *General Discussion* section above.

                  (gaze rt)   cond
- **SUPPOSE   DEAF   INDEX-*rt*,**

    This is the *condition* portion of a conditional sentence. A description of conditionals in ASL can be found in the *General Discussion* section in this unit and in Unit 10.

- **THEREABOUTS**

    When this sign is used with dates or times, it means 'approximately'. This is similar to the way some English speakers express the idea of approximate time—e.g. 'fifty-ish', 'seven-thirty-ish'.

- **FROM-*rt*-GO-TO-*lf***

    Notice that this sign moves from the location of the Gallaudet graduates (Lee's right) to the location previously assigned to Gallaudet (Lee's left).

- **STUNNED***

    Notice that this sign is stressed which makes it more emphatic. This sign also means 'dumbfounded' or 'speechless'.

<u>nodding</u>   <u>nod</u>   <u>nod</u>

Pat₅: SAME-AS MY MOTHER, GRADUATE NINETEEN FIVE NINE INDEX-*rt*,

                          <u>cs</u>   (gaze *rt*)

ONE-YEAR-PASTwg GO-TO-*rt* VISIT, SHOCK*

                            <u>cs</u>

• **ONE-YEAR-PAST**wg

> The sign **ONE-YEAR-PAST**wg is a variant of the sign **ONE-YEAR-PAST.** Compare the two illustrations below. Notice that in this dialogue the sign **ONE-YEAR-PAST**wg occurs with the non-manual signal used to convey the meaning 'close in time or space'. See Unit 11 for an explanation of this signal.

ONE-YEAR-PAST   ONE-YEAR-PASTwg

                                                               <u>cond</u>

Lee₅: "PSHAW", SUPPOSE FIFTEEN YEAR FUTURE US-TWO GO-TO-*lf* VISIT,

(gaze *lf*)

      GALLAUDET AGAIN CHANGE

                                                                              <u>cond</u>

• **SUPPOSE   FIFTEEN   YEAR   FUTURE   US-TWO   GO-TO-***lf***   VISIT,**

> This is another example of the *condition* segment of a conditional sentence in ASL. Although both of the conditionals in this dialogue (Lee₄ and Lee₅) are introduced with the sign **SUPPOSE,** conditionals do not have to be introduced by this sign. It is possible to signal a conditional with the signs **#IF** or **#IFwg** or simply by using the non-manual signal described in the *General Discussion* sections of this unit and Unit 10.

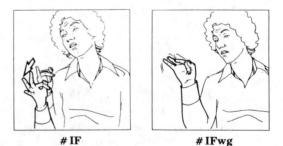

        # IF   **# IFwg**

H. Sample Drills

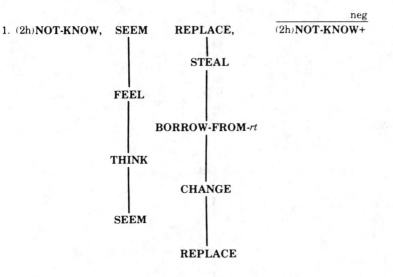

1. (2h)NOT-KNOW,   SEEM   REPLACE,   (2h)NOT-KNOW+ (neg)

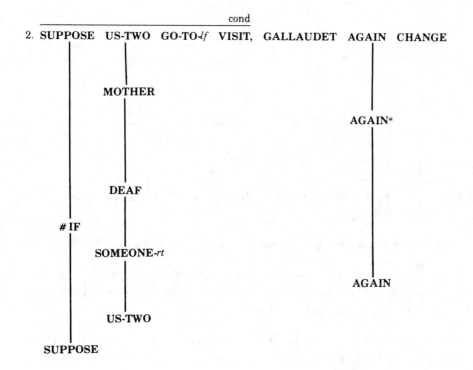

2. SUPPOSE   US-TWO   GO-TO-lf   VISIT,   GALLAUDET   AGAIN   CHANGE   (cond)

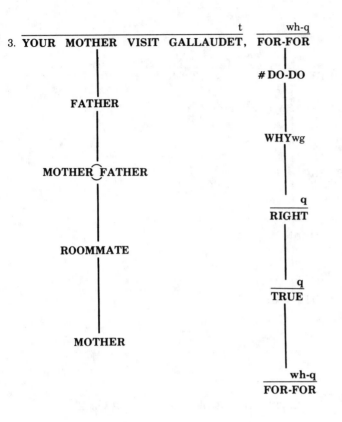

3.
$$\overline{\text{YOUR MOTHER VISIT GALLAUDET,}}^{t} \overline{\text{FOR-FOR}}^{\text{wh-q}}$$

I. Video Notes

If you have access to the videotape package designed to accompany these texts, you will notice the following:

- How both Pat and Lee gaze at Pat's hand while he signs the date 1973.

- The 'neg + q' signal that Pat uses (without any manual signs) during Lee's second turn after Lee tells him the statue isn't missing. Pat uses this combined 'neg + q' to respond 'Oh, it isn't missing?'.

- Pat's use of headnodding during his fifth turn to assert that his mother actually had the kind of experience that Lee has been describing and then to indicate that she graduated in 1959.

- The "facial sign" (sometimes called **UH-HUH** or **YEAH-I-KNOW-THAT**) that Pat uses during Lee's fifth turn to show his agreement. This sign involves a rapid, repeated wrinkling of the nose—sometimes only on one side of the nose.

Unit 20

Time

A. Synopsis

Pat and Lee are waiting outside for a friend. Pat asks if Lee is going to Europe next summer for the WFD meeting. Lee says s/he just had a two-week vacation and is broke. Lee says s/he slept every morning and fixed up the house in the afternoon. Pat's jealous because s/he hasn't had a vacation in two years. But next summer s/he is definitely going to Europe. Pat wants to travel around there and soon plans to take care of all the ticketing, scheduling, etc.

B. Cultural Information: The World Federation of the Deaf

The World Federation of the Deaf (WFD) was established in September 1951 at an international meeting in Rome, Italy. At that meeting, a constitution was adopted and officers of the international organization were elected. Among the purposes of the WFD is to provide an international forum for discussing various problems and advances in the lives of Deaf people on an international scale. The WFD also serves as a consulting body to the United Nations and has worked closely with such international organizations as UNESCO, the International Labour Organization, and the World Health Organization.

At the present time, there are 57 national organizations of Deaf people who are members of the WFD. The WFD has a number of commissions which focus on various aspects of deafness and the lives of Deaf people. Some of those commissions are: Art and Culture, Communications, Pedagogy, Psychology, and Social Aspects of Deafness.

The WFD has international meetings every four years in different countries throughout the world. For example, the VIIth World Congress of the WFD was held in Washington, D.C. in 1975. The theme of that Congress was "Full Citizenship for All Deaf People". In 1979, the VIIIth World Congress of the WFD was held in Varna, Bulgaria. The theme of that Congress was "The Deaf People in Modern Society". At the 1979 Congress, Dragojub Vukotic from Belgrade, Yugoslavia was elected President of the WFD. For further information about the WFD, contact: National Association of the Deaf, 814 Thayer Avenue, Silver Spring, Md. 20910.

C. Dialogue

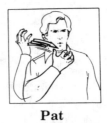

Pat

Pat_1:
$$\overline{\text{co}} \hspace{5.5cm} \overline{\hspace{1cm}\text{q}}$$
"HEY", ONE-YEAR-FUTURE SUMMER EUROPE GO-*rt* YOU

Pat_2:
$$\overline{\hspace{4.5cm}\text{t}}$$
KNOW-THAT MEETING W-F-D, EUROPE ONE-YEAR-FUTURE SUMMER

Pat_3:
$$\overline{\hspace{1.5cm}\text{t}} \hspace{1cm} \overline{\hspace{1.5cm}\text{wh-q}}$$
VACATION, (2h)#DO-DO
$$\hspace{4cm}\textit{YOU}$$

Pat_4:
$$\hspace{3cm}\overline{\hspace{3cm}\text{t}} \hspace{1.5cm} \overline{\hspace{1cm}\text{neg}}$$
JEALOUS ME, UP-TIL-NOW* TWO YEAR, VACATION (2h)NONE

Pat_5:
$$\hspace{2cm}\overline{\hspace{4.5cm}\text{t}} \hspace{2cm} \overline{\hspace{1.5cm}\text{nodding}}$$
RIGHT++, ONE-YEAR-FUTURE SUMMER W-F-D, ME GO-*rt* DECIDE* FINISH*

Pat_6:
$$\hspace{2.5cm}\overline{\hspace{2cm}\text{t}} \hspace{4.5cm} \overline{\hspace{1.5cm}\text{nodding}}$$
(2h)WANTwg, FEW-DAY-FUTURE, PLAN TICKET, TIME, SCHEDULE ALL-INCLUSIVE

Lee

$$\text{Lee}_1:\quad \overline{\text{EUROPE} \quad \text{FOR-FOR}}^{\text{wh-q}}$$

$$\text{Lee}_2:\quad \overline{\text{MONEY}}^{\text{neg}} \quad \text{TWO-WEEK} \quad \text{VACATION} \quad \overline{\text{RECENT}}^{\text{cs}} \quad \text{(2h)BROKE} \quad \text{ME}$$

$$\text{Lee}_3:\quad \text{EVERY-MORNING} \quad \text{SLEEP,} \quad \overline{\text{WORK,}}^{\text{t}} \quad \overline{\text{(2h)NONE,}}^{\text{neg}} \quad \overline{\text{EARLY-AFTERNOON} \quad \text{(2h)\# FIX+,}}^{\text{t}} \quad \text{HOUSE}$$

$$\text{Lee}_4:\quad \text{BLAME} \overset{\frown}{} \text{YOURSELF*,} \quad \overline{\text{POSTPONE}}^{\text{th}}\textit{"long time"}$$

$$\text{Lee}_5:\quad \overline{\text{TRAVEL-AROUND}}^{(\underline{\quad\text{puff cheeks}\quad})} \quad \overline{\text{\#WILL} \quad \text{YOU}}^{\text{q}}$$

D. Key Illustrations

Pat

MEETING

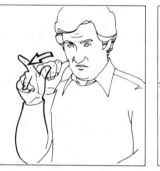

ONE-YEAR-FUTURE

(2h)# DO-DO

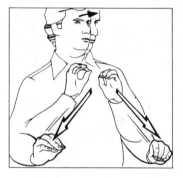

(2h)NONE

FEW-DAY-FUTURE

ALL-INCLUSIVE

Lee

RECENT

(2h)BROKE

EVERY-MORNING

(2h)NONE   BLAME◡YOURSELF   POSTPONE*"long time"*

E. Supplementary Illustrations

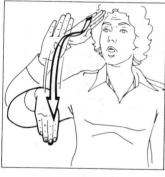

KNOW-THAT

(2h)#FIX-*arc*

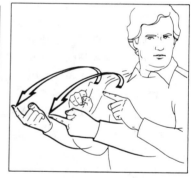

UP-TIL-NOW

TRAVEL-AROUND

#WILL   WANTwg

F. General Discussion: Time

The previous discussions of time in Units 2 and 11 provided an introduction to a number of different features of ASL—e.g. the *time line,* how some time signs can incorporate numbers, ways of indicating "regularity" and "duration" with time signs, and some non-manual signals relating to time. This discussion will expand on some of this information as well as describe how some time signs can be modulated to express the concept of "repetition and duration".

In Unit 2, the discussion of the *time line* pointed out that the direction of movement of a time sign indicates its relation to present time. This can be seen in the two illustrations below.

FEW-DAY-FUTURE   FEW-DAY-PAST

There are some time signs which use the *time line,* but use the passive hand instead of the body as the point of reference. Thus, in the illustration below, the active hand indicates time in relation to the passive hand—which can represent any time (e.g. today, last month, two years from now). Some other signs like this are **BEFORE, AFTER, NEXT, UNTIL, POSTPONE,** and **PREPONE** ('move backward in time').

FROM-NOW-ON

The handshape of certain time signs can be changed so that the Signer can indicate a specific number of time units. When Signers do this, they are incorporating a number into the time sign. For example, a Signer can convey the meaning 'three months' by incorporating the handshape which represents the number '3' into the sign **(ONE)-MONTH.**

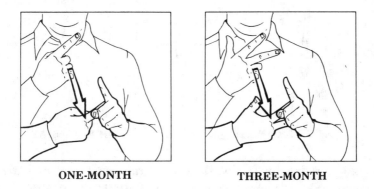

ONE-MONTH   THREE-MONTH

This type of *number incorporation* also occurs with units of money (e.g. **FIVE-CENT**), clock time (e.g. **THREE-O'CLOCK**), and age (e.g. **AGE-SEVEN**). Numbers of dollars can also be indicated by maintaining the same movement, but changing the handshape (e.g. **THREE-DOLLAR, SEVEN-DOLLAR**).

THREE-O'CLOCK   AGE-SEVEN   AGE-THREE

Number incorporated time signs can be moved in relation to the *time line.*

TWO-WEEK   TWO-WEEK-PAST   TWO-WEEK-FUTURE

Certain time signs can also be changed to express the concept of *regularity*. For example, the sign **MONDAY** can be changed (modulated) to express the meaning 'every Monday' or 'every other Monday'.

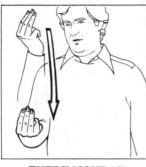
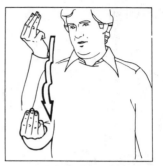

EVERY-MONDAY   EVERY-OTHER-MONDAY

Whereas signs for days of the week express the concept of *regularity* with a sweeping downward movement, signs like **EVERY-MORNING, EVERY-AFTERNOON,** and **EVERY-NIGHT** do this with a sweeping, horizontal movement. Other signs, like **EVERY-ONE-WEEK, EVERY-ONE-MONTH,** and **EVERY-ONE-YEAR,** express the concept of *regularity* with fast repetition of the sign. Notice that these modulated signs can also incorporate numbers (e.g. **EVERY-TWO-YEAR**). Some Signers will also move them in accordance with the *time line* (e.g. **EVERY-ONE-MONTH-FUTURE**).

EVERY-MORNING   EVERY-TWO-YEAR   EVERY-ONE-MONTH-FUTURE

Some time signs can be changed to express the concept of *duration*. For example, the signs **DAY** and **MORNING** can be changed to express the meanings 'all day' and 'all morning', respectively. The Signer's facial behaviors (e.g. *'puff.cheeks'* or *'intense'*) also indicate the length of time and/or the Signer's feelings about the duration.

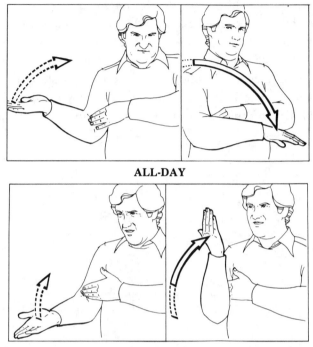

ALL-DAY

ALL-MORNING

The concept of *approximate/relative time* is often expressed by using the sign **THEREABOUTS** (illustrated in Unit 22) immediately after a time sign(s) — e.g. **TWO-O'CLOCK THEREABOUTS; MONDAY TUESDAY THEREABOUTS.** However, some time signs can be changed to express this concept without using the sign **THEREABOUTS.** For example, the signs **MORNING** and **AFTERNOON** (and other signs for periods of the day) can express this concept by shaking the active hand up and down in a relaxed way. Similarly, meanings like 'about two o'clock' or 'two-ish' can be expressed by shaking the number handshape back and forth in a relaxed manner.

SOMETIME-IN-THE-MORNING   SOMETIME-IN-THE-AFTERNOON

The form of some signs can also be changed to express the concept of a repeated and long period of time. For example, the sign **ONE-WEEK** can be changed to express the meaning 'for weeks and weeks'; the sign **ONE-MONTH** can be changed to express the meaning 'for months and months'. These signs are changed so that they have a slow, intense movement (which shows *duration*) combined with a repeated movement (which shows *repetition* or *regularity*).

In general, the active hand makes a straight-line movement toward the passive hand, followed by a slow, intense movement during which time the active hand arcs back to where the straight movement began. These movements can be seen in the following illustrations in which the dotted lines indicate the slow, intense movement. This cycle is repeated (usually twice) and is often accompanied by a rocking movement of the head/body and an intense opening and closing of the mouth.

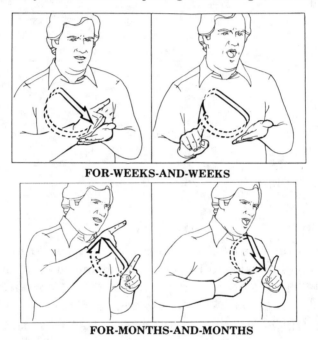

FOR-WEEKS-AND-WEEKS

FOR-MONTHS-AND-MONTHS

Notice that the same type of movement and facial behavior can occur with the sign **SAME-OLD-THING** (Unit 11). Try using this movement with the signs **YEAR** or **MONDAY** to express the meanings 'for years and years' or 'Monday after Monday after Monday'.

SAME-OLD-THING

Facial expression and other non-manual behaviors can also indicate time in ASL. The 'cs' signal described in Unit 11 expresses the concept of 'closeness to the present time or space'. This signal can be seen in the photos below.

cs
───
NOW

cs
───
NOW

Notice that, although both Signers are expressing the meaning 'right now' or 'just this very moment', their facial behavior is slightly different. The 'cs' signal used by the male Signer is more intense than the 'cs' signal used by the female Signer. It also appears on both sides of the male Signer's face whereas the female Signer's 'cs' signal is stronger on the right side of her face. (Also notice the variation in handshape for the sign **NOW**.) When the 'cs' signal is used with time signs like **NOW** or **ONE-DAY-PAST,** it functions as an adverb and emphasizes their closeness to present time. It also functions as an adverb with signs that indicate location like **FRONT** or **HERE,** meaning 'very close to' that location—e.g. 'right in front' or 'right here'.

The 'cs' signal can also occur with verbs. In these cases, it indicates that something just happened or is about to happen soon. The following photos convey the meaning 'just arrived'. Again, notice that the 'cs' signal is more intense for the male Signer than for the female Signer.

cs
─────
ARRIVE-AT-*here*

cs
─────
ARRIVE-AT-*here*

Just as the Signer's facial behavior can indicate 'closeness in time or space', it can also indicate 'distance in time or space'. One way in which Signers can show that something is 'far away' is to use the *'puff.cheeks'* signal. This signal conveys the meanings 'a lot; huge number of; large; huge; of great magnitude'. Another way of showing distance in time or space is the *'intense'* signal. This signal conveys the meanings 'awfully large; surprisingly huge; of awfully great magnitude; to an unusually large degree'. Compare these two signals in the illustrations below.

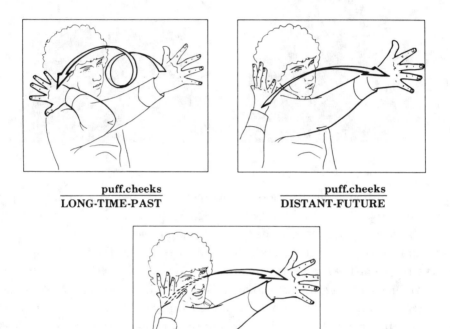

<table>
<tr><td align="center">**puff.cheeks**
LONG-TIME-PAST</td><td align="center">**puff.cheeks**
DISTANT-FUTURE</td></tr>
</table>

intense
DISTANT-FUTURE*

The illustration at the top right shows that something will occur 'far into the future' while the one below it shows that something will happen 'awfully far into the future'. Notice that the manual portion of the sign with the *'intense'* signal is stressed—the dotted lines mean that the movement was slower during that part of the sign.

These two signals can also be used in other contexts with signs other than time signs. They can be used to express the Signer's feelings about the amount, size, or degree of something. Although the meanings of the *'puff.cheeks'* and *'intense'* signals are similar, the *'intense'* signal seems to indicate that the amount, size, or degree is much greater than expected. Some Signers say that when they use the *'intense'* signal, they have a negative feeling about the thing's size, shape, etc.—like, it's too large, too many, too far, etc.

Compare the following photos to help you clearly distinguish the two signals. (The sign shown below is also sometimes glossed as **HORDES-OF.**)

puff.cheeks
SCADS-OF

puff.cheeks
SCADS-OF

intense
SCADS-OF

intense
SCADS-OF

This section has reviewed a wide variety of ways in which ASL Signers communicate information about time. Many time signs are produced in relation to the *time line*, using either the Signer's body or passive hand as the point of reference. A variety of signs incorporate numbers in order to indicate specific time periods. Some of the time signs can be used to express concepts of regularity, duration, approximate time, and prolonged, repeated time. Several non-manual signals can also be used to express the concepts 'closeness to' or 'distance from' present time or space.

Another major way in which Signers communicate information about time (duration or frequency) is by using various verb modulations which indicate what is called *temporal aspect*. These modulations are described in Units 8, 17, and 26.

G. Text Analysis

Pat$_1$: "HEY"^{co}, ONE-YEAR-FUTURE SUMMER EUROPE GO-*rt* YOU^{q}

- **"HEY"** (co)

  This is an example of a conversation opener in ASL. A discussion of conversation openers and other conversation behaviors can be found in the Introduction to Units 10-18.

- **ONE-YEAR-FUTURE SUMMER EUROPE GO-*rt* YOU** (q)

  Notice that this sentence is a 'yes-no' question, indicated by the *'q'* signal and also a reference to the Addressee (**YOU**) at the end of the question.

  Also notice that the time signs occur at the beginning of the sentence and that the sign **ONE-YEAR-FUTURE** moves forward 'into the future'.

Lee$_1$: EUROPE FOR-FOR (wh-q)

This sentence is a 'wh-word' question. See Units 1, 10, or 19 for a description of the non-manual behaviors which accompany this type of question.

Pat$_2$: KNOW-THAT MEETING W-F-D (t), EUROPE ONE-YEAR-FUTURE SUMMER

- **KNOW-THAT MEETING W-F-D,** (t)

  This is an example of a topic. In general, the sign **KNOW-THAT** (or sometimes **YOU KNOW**) is used when the Signer thinks that the Addressee is familiar with the topic. The non-manual behaviors used to indicate a topic are described in Units 1, 10, and 19.

Lee$_2$: (neg) MONEY TWO-WEEK VACATION RECENT (cs) (2h)BROKE ME

- neg

  Lee responds negatively to Pat's initial question (after first obtaining some clarifying information) by using non-manual behaviors which signal negation. Units 1, 10, and 19 provide a description of these behaviors.

- **TWO-WEEK**

    Notice that the Signer incorporates the number **TWO** into this sign.

  <u>   cs</u>
- **RECENT**

    Here the Signer not only uses the sign **RECENT,** but also uses the *'cs'* signal to emphasize that the vacation occurred 'very recently'. A description of the *'cs'* signal can be found in Units 10 and 19.

<u> t</u>   <u>   wh-q</u>
Pat₃: VACATION, (2h)**#DO-DO**
          YOU

      <u>   wh-q</u>
- **(2h)# DO-DO**
      YOU

    The sign **# DO-DO** is a fingerspelled loan sign. In this context it conveys the meaning 'what did you do?'. However, if the sign is produced with palms down and then moved in small horizontal circles, it means 'to have to do many things', 'to be involved with busy work'.

    Notice that the non-manual *'wh-q'* signal occurs throughout the question. Also notice that the sign **YOU** occurs at the end of the question and is made with the left hand.

<u> t</u> <u> neg</u>   <u>   t</u>
Lee₃: EVERY-MORNING SLEEP, WORK, (2h)NONE, EARLY-AFTERNOON (2h)**# FIX+** , HOUSE

- **EVERY-MORNING**

    This is an example of a sign which uses a horizontal 'sweep' to indicate regularity. See the *General Discussion* section above or Unit 11 for further information.

      <u> neg</u>
- **(2h)NONE**

    Notice that the Signer uses the non-manual behaviors for expressing negation with this negation sign. Also notice that the Signer uses the two-handed variant of the sign

NONE. In this informal context, the Signer instead could have used one of the following signs:

NONE

NONE
(emphatic)

NONE
(colloquial)

Also notice how the negation sign functions as the *comment* after the *topic* **WORK.**

- **(2h)# FIX+**

   This is another example of a fingerspelled loan sign in ASL. In this case, the Signer uses the two-handed variant and repeats the sign (in a different location) to show that s/he was working on more than one thing in the house.

t

neg

Pat₄: JEALOUS   ME,   UP-TIL-NOW*   TWO   YEAR,   VACATION   (2h)NONE

- **UP-TIL-NOW***

   The sign **UP-TIL-NOW*** moves in accordance with the *time line,* moving from 'the past' to 'the present'. Notice also that it is stressed. This means that the initial portion of the sign is slower and more deliberate.

th

Lee₄: BLAME‿YOURSELF*,   POSTPONE"*long time*"

- **BLAME‿YOURSELF***

   This is an example of a verb which can indicate its object (and sometimes its subject). See Units 4, 13, and 22 for further information on verbs of this type.

Notice that this is also an example of two signs which act together like a single sign. In this case, the handshape used in the two signs is the same. This helps to make the two signs seem like a single sign.

$$\overline{\text{th}}$$
• **POSTPONE**"*long time*"

This is an example of a time sign which uses the passive hand as the reference point. The active hand then moves forward 'into the future' from the passive hand. Similarly, if the active hand moved backwards from the passive hand 'toward the present', it would mean that the activity or event is moved up in time—i.e. occurs earlier than was originally scheduled. This latter movement has led to coining the English word "prepone" as a gloss for the sign.

Notice that the sign is accompanied by the non-manual signal *'th'* which can mean 'carelessly' or 'without paying attention'. Notice also that the sign is produced with a repeated, slow elliptical movement which indicates that something has happened 'for a long time'. Units 8, 17, and 26 provide a more detailed description of how ASL Signers modulate verbs to show temporal aspect.

$$\overline{\text{t}}\qquad\overline{\text{nodding}}$$
Pat₅: RIGHT++, ONE-YEAR-FUTURE SUMMER W-F-D, ME GO-*rt* DECIDE* FINISH*

$$\qquad\qquad\qquad\qquad\overline{\text{nodding}}$$
• **ME   GO**-*rt*   **DECIDE***   **FINISH***

This is the *comment* portion of the sentence. It makes a comment about the event cited in the topic. Notice that the signs **DECIDE** and **FINISH** are both stressed to emphasize the Signer's intent. Notice also that the sign **FINISH** is accompanied by headnodding—which is used to assert the truth or validity of what the Signer is saying.

$$\overline{(\text{puff cheeks})}\text{q}$$
Lee₅: TRAVEL-AROUND   #WILL   YOU

$$\qquad\qquad\qquad\overline{(\text{puff.cheeks})}$$
• **TRAVEL-AROUND**

Notice that this sign is accompanied by the non-manual signal *'puff.cheeks'* to indicate 'a lot of' or 'a great deal of'. The *General Discussion* section contains further information about this signal as well as photos of it.

• **#WILL**

This is another fingerspelled loan sign.

nodding

Pat₆: (2h)WANTwg,   FEW-DAY-FUTURE,   PLAN   TICKET,   TIME,   SCHEDULE   ALL-INCLUSIVE

- **(2h)WANTwg**

    This sign is a two-handed variant of the sign **WANT**. Compare the two illustrations below. Both of these variants can be produced with one or two hands.

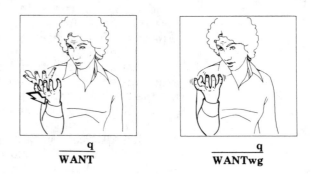

q	q
WANT	WANTwg

- **FEW-DAY-FUTURE**

    This is another example of a sign which moves forward 'into the future' in accordance with the *time line*. Notice also that it is accompanied by the non-manual behaviors which indicate it is serving as a topic in the sentence.

- **ALL-INCLUSIVE**

    This is another case in which the Signer uses *'nodding'* to stress the truth or validity of the statement. Here the Signer uses this signal to assert that *everything* will be settled in the next few days.

H. Sample Drills

<u>   t   </u>   <u>   nodding   </u>

1. FEW-DAY-FUTURE, PLAN TICKET, TIME, SCHEDULE ALL-INCLUSIVE

   ONE-WEEK-FUTURE

   THREE-WEEK-PAST

   TWO-YEAR-PASTwg

   FEW-DAY-PAST

   TWO-WEEK-FUTURE

   ONE-DAY-FUTURE

   ONE-YEAR-FUTURE

   ONE-WEEK-PAST

   FEW-DAY-FUTURE

                                <u> t </u>   <u> neg </u>   <u> t </u>

2. EVERY-MORNING SLEEP, WORK, (2h)NONE, EARLY-AFTERNOON (2h)#FIX+, HOUSE

   EVERY-NIGHT

                                                 EVERY-AFTERNOON

   EVERY-DAY

                                                 EVERY-NIGHT

   EVERY-MORNING

                                                 NOON

   MIDNIGHT

                                     SOMETIME-IN-THE-AFTERNOON

   ALL-MORNING

                                                 ALL-NIGHT

   EVERY-MORNING

                                                 EARLY-AFTERNOON

$$\overline{\qquad\qquad\qquad\qquad\qquad}^{\,t}\ \ \overline{\qquad\qquad\qquad}^{\,th}$$

3. BLAME YOURSELF*, UP-TIL-NOW TWO YEAR, POSTPONE*"long time"*

ALL-WEEK

|

EVERY-MONDAY

|

EVERY-MORNING

|

ALL-MONTH

|

THREE-MONTH

|

EVERY-FRIDAY

|

FIVE YEAR

|

EVERY-NIGHT

TWO YEAR

I. Video Notes

If you have access to the videotape package designed to accompany these texts, you will notice the following:

- How the *'cs'* signal in Lee's second turn is much 'weaker' than in the illustrations found in the *General Discussion* section.

- How Lee's eyes follow the two different locations of the loan sign (2h)# **FIX+** during his third turn.

- How each of the fingerspelled loan signs that appear in the dialogue (# **DO-DO**, # **FIX**, # **WILL**) look like regular signs, rather than fingerspelled words.

- The clear illustration of the non-manual adverb *'th'* in Lee's fifth turn. Also notice how Lee's non-focused gaze 'agrees with' the meaning of the adverb.

- The modulation *"long time"* which occurs with the verb **POSTPONE** in Lee's fifth turn. Unlike the drawing, the verb here is repeated several times.

- In Pat's last turn, how she definitely pauses between each 'item' on her 'list' of planned activities.

- How Pat's sign **ALL-INCLUSIVE** during her last turn differs from the illustration. Notice how this sign is similar to the sign often glossed as **INCLUDE** or **INVOLVE**.

Unit 21

Pronominalization

A. Synopsis

Lee has just gotten a new TTY and is using it in the lounge to make a phone call. Pat asks if Lee has called ⚠ to let him/her know about the new TTY—because if it breaks down, ⚠ is really good at fixing TTYs. Lee asks if ⚠ has ever fixed Pat's TTY. Pat responds positively and comments that ⚠ gets the work done really fast. Lee decides to call ⚠ tomorrow.

B. Cultural Information: Telecommunication Devices

Just as wake-up alarms and other signaling devices have been adapted for use by members of the Deaf Community, it should not be surprising that devices have been developed which make it possible for deaf persons to use the telephone. These Telecommunication Devices for the Deaf (TDD) make it possible for individuals with such units to type messages back and forth to each other using regular telephone lines. Some of these devices provide paper printouts ("hard copy"); however, many of them use only a light display where the characters move from right to left and then disappear off the display ("soft copy"). Currently there are about ten different types of TDDs.

Because the first telecommunication devices were actually Western Union teletypewriters (TTYs) with phone couplers, the acronym TTY has become a generic term used by deaf people to refer to telecommunication devices in general. Some people use the term "MCM" to refer to any portable device that gives "soft copy" since the MCM was among the first such units to be marketed. The advantage of a TTY is that it offers "hard copy" which can be filed for later use and which means the person does not have to constantly watch the display as the message is typed out. However, TTYs are generally not portable. MCMs, which provide "soft copy", are generally portable and can be taken on trips, to meetings, etc.

There are certain *rules* that people generally follow when using a TTY or an MCM: always identify yourself ("PAT JONES HERE" or "THIS IS PAT JONES") since you generally cannot tell who a person is by how s/he types; when you want the other person to respond, type GA ("THIS IS PAT JONES GA") so that the other person knows it is his/her turn to G̲o A̲head; when you are done with your conversation, type SK or GA ("SEE YOU TOMORROW SK or GA") so the person can decide to stop (SK = "Stop Key") or continue to respond (GA); conversations are ended by typing SKSK.

Obviously, it takes longer to type than to talk on the phone. For this reason, deaf people have been trying to obtain reduced phone rates, especially for long distance calls. Several states have, in fact, reduced phone rates for deaf people with TTYs.

Since not every deaf person has a TTY or an MCM, an International Telephone Directory of the Deaf is published periodically. In 1976, there were over 5,000 people listed in the directory. More and more hospitals, police and fire stations, banks, travel agencies, consumer agencies, etc., are also beginning to purchase and use TDDs. Generally, places and individuals who have TDDs will provide a phone number and some indication of this fact—e.g. #123-4567 (voice or TTY). For more information, contact: Telecom for the Deaf, 814 Thayer Avenue, Silver Spring, Md. 20910.

C. Dialogue

Pat

Pat₁:
```
              co                                                q
        ————————————  ————————————————————————————————————————————
        THAT-ONE-rt   T-T-Y   YOUR↔POSS-rt
"HEY"
```

Pat₂:
```
        nodding                    (gaze rt                    )   (nodding   )q
        ———————  ————————————————————————————————————————————   ——————————————
                 FINISH  you-TTY-CALL-TO-rt  you-INFORM-rt ⃤ ,  FINISH⌢YOU
             YOU
```

Pat₃:
```
                     (gaze rt        )cond                            q
        ————————————————————————————————  ————————————————————————————
        SUPPOSE   T-T-Y   BREAK-DOWN,    YOURSELF   FIX   QMwg
```

Pat₄:
```
                             t                        nodding
                ——————————————————                 ——————————————
                ⃤   INDEX-rt,  FIX+   SKILL*   POSS+ -rt
"UMMM"
```

Pat₅:
```
        nodding                                    nodding
        ——————                                     ——————————
        FAST   WORK   REALLY-ADEPT   INDEX-rt
```

Lee

Lee₁:
<u>nodding</u>   <u>   cs</u>
NEW,   RECENT ARRIVE-*here*

Lee₂: <u>   t</u>   <u>   wh-q</u>
INFORM-*lf*  , **FOR-FOR**
                                 "WHAT"

Lee₃: **SILLY⌢ YOU,**

     ME *me*-**SUMMON**-*rt* **SOMEONE**-*rt* (2h)**FROM**-*rt*-**COME-TO**-*here* (2h)**#FIX*** (2h)**"WELL"**

Lee₄: <u>   q</u>
OH-I-SEE   **YOUR T-T-Y #FIX FINISH INDEX**-*lf* **QMwg**

Lee₅: <u>nodding</u>
  OH-I-SEE FINE, **ONE-DAY-FUTURE ME** *me*-**TTY-CALL-TO**-*lf*

D. Key Illustrations

Pat

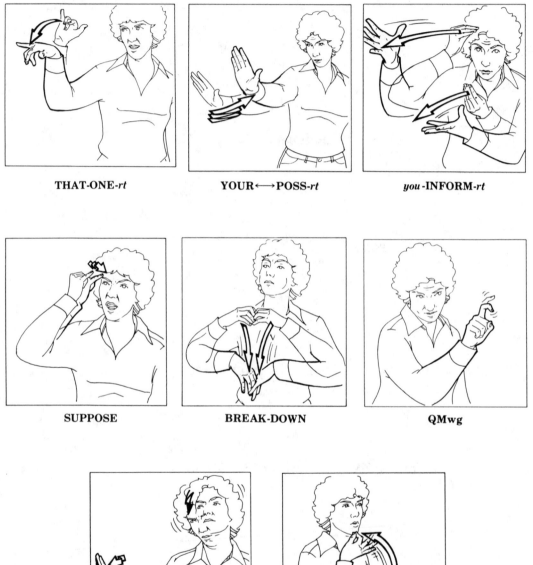

THAT-ONE-*rt*   YOUR⟷POSS-*rt*   *you* -INFORM-*rt*

SUPPOSE   BREAK-DOWN   QMwg

POSS+ -*rt*   REALLY-ADEPT

Lee

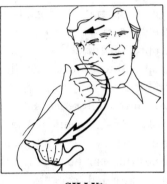

SILLY*

E. Supplementary Illustrations

you-TTY-CALL-TO-*rt*   SOMEONE-*rt*   OH-I-SEE

F. General Discussion: Pronominalization

The discussions of pronominalization in Units 3 and 12 introduced several types of pronominal reference: indexic, possessive, reflexive/emphatic, and demonstrative. They also focused on strategies for discerning *where* to 'point' (including the "reality principle") and on ways to assign spatial locations to persons, places, or things. It will be helpful to review these discussions before proceeding. This Unit will expand upon some of the information provided in these previous units as well as introduce additional ways of assigning spatial locations, including ways to use the non-dominant hand to set up referents.

As described previously, pronominal reference in ASL generally involves 'pointing' to an actual person/place/thing that is "present" in the area of the communication or to a spatial location which has been assigned to that person/place/thing. There are about nine different handshapes that can be used for pronominal reference in ASL. By far, the most common is the extended index finger, or '1' handshape (e.g. **YOU**). Others are the flat hand with fingers together (e.g. **YOUR**), the closed fist (e.g. **MYSELF**), the closed hand with thumb and pinky extended (e.g. **THAT-ONE**-*rt*), the semi-open hand with fingers together (e.g. honorific **YOU**), and four handshapes that are used exclusively for plural reference: '2' (or the variant shown in Unit 3), '3', '4', and '5'. In informal contexts, some Signers will also use a closed fist handshape with thumb extended and will point with the thumb (e.g. **THUMB-INDEX**-*rt*). Finally, eye gaze (usually accompanied by a slight brow raise and head nod or tilt) can also be used as a form of pronominal reference.

The handshape that the Signer uses determines the type of pronominal reference. For example, in the two illustrations below, the handshape on the left indicates that the pronoun is *indexic* (meaning 'we') while the handshape on the right indicates that the pronoun is *reflexive/emphatic* (meaning 'ourselves').

WE   **OURSELVES**
(other referents not present)   (other referents not present)

Similarly, 'pointing' with the palm of the handshape illustrated below indicates the pronoun is *possessive*. To refer to more than one person or thing, the Signer will either point to each location separately or will use a 'sweep' of the hand across those locations.

YOUR (plural)

The possessive pronoun can also be used to show ownership or ask about ownership in another way. When the thing that is owned is present in the communication area (e.g. a book), the Signer may choose to reference both the owner *and* the owned thing with the possessive pronoun. For example, suppose the Signer sees a new book on her friend's desk. To ask whether the book belongs to her friend, she might use the sign illustrated below.

$$\overline{\hspace{3cm}}^{q}$$

YOUR ⟷ POSS-*book*

When the handshape used for possessive reference repeatedly points toward someone, it can also mean that something is a 'characteristic of' or a 'trait of' that particular person (or sometimes, an animal or thing). For example, in the sentence below, the repetition of the possessive pronoun toward 'Lee' (located to the right) indicates that he is 'characteristically clumsy'.

$$\overline{\text{th+t}} \qquad\qquad \overline{\text{nodding}}$$
AWKWARD, L-E-E-*rt* **POSS-***lee*++

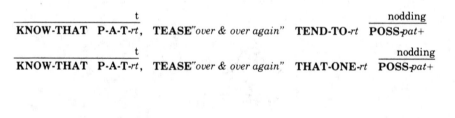

POSS-*rt*++
'characteristically'

When talking about a character trait of a person, etc., the repeated possessive pronoun is sometimes preceded by the sign **TEND-TO** or the sign **THAT-ONE**. This is seen in the two examples below, both of which basically mean 'Pat's a real teaser'.

$$\overline{\qquad\qquad\quad\text{t}\qquad\qquad\quad} \qquad\qquad\qquad\qquad\qquad \overline{\text{nodding}}$$
KNOW-THAT P-A-T-*rt*, **TEASE**"*over & over again*" **TEND-TO-***rt* **POSS-***pat*+

$$\overline{\qquad\qquad\quad\text{t}\qquad\qquad\quad} \qquad\qquad\qquad\qquad\qquad \overline{\text{nodding}}$$
KNOW-THAT P-A-T-*rt*, **TEASE**"*over & over again*" **THAT-ONE-***rt* **POSS-***pat*+

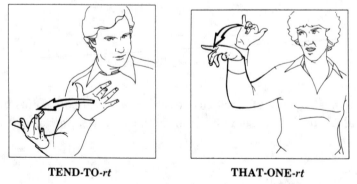

TEND-TO-*rt*   **THAT-ONE-***rt*

Sometimes when the Signer uses either of these two signs with the possessive pronoun, their form changes in the way illustrated below. When this happens, the two signs look and act like a single sign. Notice that the possessive pronoun is no longer repeated and that the head nod accompanies both 'joined' signs.

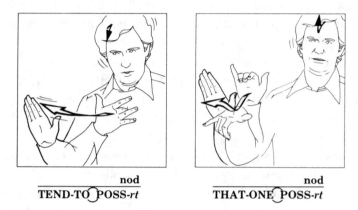

<table>
<tr><td style="text-align:center">nod
TEND-TO POSS-rt</td><td style="text-align:center">nod
THAT-ONE POSS-rt</td></tr>
</table>

There are many different ways to assign spatial locations to persons or things that are not present in the communication area. Unit 3 listed several principles which are helpful in learning how to use those locations once they have been established. Unit 12 described various strategies for deciding *where* to establish each person or thing. The reader is encouraged to review those principles and strategies. What follows is a brief description of various ways that a 'non-present' person, place, or thing can be given a spatial location. Although these ways are described separately here, in actual conversation, several of them may (and often do) occur together.

One way to assign a spatial location to a person, etc., is to make the sign for that referent in a particular location. For example, in Unit 4, Lee assigned a location on the left to the 'two brothers' and a location on the right to the 'one sister' by making the sign **BROTHER** (and **TWO**) to the left and the sign **SISTER** (and **ONE**) to the right. Similarly, Pat in Unit 16 established 'signed languages' on the right and 'spoken languages' on the left by making the signs for those referents in those locations. A related way is to fingerspell the name of the person, etc., in a particular location—or make the name sign in a particular location, as seen in Unit 1 when Pat established △ to the left during his/her third turn.

Another way to assign a spatial location to a person, etc., is to use a pronoun which 'points to' a particular location after making the sign for that person. For example, in Pat's third turn in Unit 1, s/he indexed a location on the right after signing **SUPERINTENDENT.** This clearly assigned that location to the 'superintendent'. Similarly, Lee in Unit 3 assigned a location to △ by signing **US-TWO**-*rt,* and Pat in Unit 12 assigned a location on the right to the 'short woman with black hair' by signing **THAT-ONE INDEX**-*rt.* Sometimes the pronoun need not occur immediately after the sign for the person, etc., as long as it is still clear who or what is the referent. For example, see how the 'mother' is established on the left during Pat's third turn in Unit 4.

Another way to assign a spatial location to something is to use a classifier for that thing in a particular location. For example, in Unit 5, Pat assigns a location to his/ her 'car' on the right by signing **3→CL@**rt. Similarly, the 'trophy' in Unit 6 is assigned a location on Lee's right by signing **A-CL@**rt. Then Lee uses his/her non-dominant hand to assign the location of the 'cup' relative to the 'trophy'— *C-CL@rt,cntr'cup behind trophy'*.

Another way to assign a spatial location to something is to use a directional verb when it is clear who or what is the referent. For example, in Pat's fourth turn (Unit 2), s/he signed **CAN   GO-TO-**rt   **MEETING.** This effectively assigned the location on Pat's right to the 'NAD meetings'—which Lee then used during his/her fourth turn: **ME   GO-TO-**lf   **ONCE-IN-AWHILE.**

Finally, head, eye, and body movements are frequently used with each of the above ways for establishing referents in space. For example, Pat looked to the left when s/he assigned that location to △ in Unit 1. Similarly, Pat in Unit 10 looked at each location as s/he assigned locations to the three groups of people who went to the Chicago NSSLRT.

More examples of each of these ways to assign spatial locations can be found throughout Units 1-27 in the *Dialogues* and *Text Analysis* sections.

Signers can also take advantage of the fact that they have two hands by using the fingers on one hand (the non-dominant hand) to represent different referents. These referents may be persons or places or things or events. This use of the non-dominant hand is very common when *listing* things—e.g. the people invited to a party, the entrance requirements to a school, or the errands scheduled for a particular day. Units 7, 14, 25, and 27 provide examples of this type of listing behavior.

Referents are established on the non-dominant hand either by (a) pointing with the dominant hand to a particular finger on the non-dominant hand (usually starting with the thumb) and then signing or fingerspelling the referent, or by (b) raising the first non-dominant finger (with an emphatic outward movement) and then signing or finger-spelling the referent with the dominant hand, successively adding one more finger on the non-dominant hand as each referent is named. Up to ten referents can be established on the non-dominant hand by using various handshapes to represent the numbers 1-10 (shaking the thumb for the tenth referent to distinguish it from the first referent).

As seen in the dialogues, once spatial locations have been assigned to persons, places, or things, they generally do not change. So each reference to that person, etc., will make use of the same location. However, this is not always the case. Sometimes a 'new' person, etc., pre-empts or takes over the location previously assigned to something else. This may happen when the topic shifts and/or a location is no longer needed for the 'old' person, etc. For example, in Unit 10, Pat assigned a particular location to the 'California meeting'. But then Lee began to talk about the 'Chicago meeting' and used that same location. From then on, the conversation focused on the Chicago meeting. There was no need for a separate location for the 'California meeting'; the 'Chicago meeting' took over that location.

Sometimes the same referent may change its location. This often happens in narratives when a character or thing moves. It also happens when the Signer shifts his/her 'perspective' (somewhat like the difference between a long-shot and a close-up in a film). For example, suppose the Signer is describing the first time he went to visit a friend's house. When first describing the house, he might locate it to his right. However, he probably would shift his perspective when he arrived at the house and knocked on the door. Now the house would move to "center stage". This shift in perspective is illustrated below.

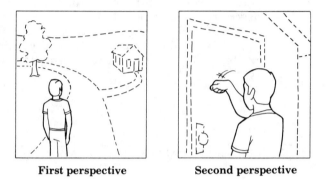

First perspective   **Second perspective**

Learning to discern how and where referents are established in space and how their locations may change is vital to effective communication in ASL.

G. Text Analysis

Pat$_1$:
$$\overline{\quad\text{co}\quad}\qquad\overline{\qquad\qquad\qquad\qquad\qquad\qquad\text{q}}$$
        "HEY"   **THAT-ONE-*rt*   T-T-Y   YOUR↔POSS-*rt***

$$\overline{\qquad\qquad\qquad\qquad\qquad\qquad\qquad\qquad\text{q}}$$
• **THAT-ONE-*rt*   T-T-Y   YOUR←→POSS-*rt***

> The sign **THAT-ONE-*rt*** is a demonstrative pronoun. See the *General Discussion* section of Unit 12 for more information on pronouns of this type.
>
> **T-T-Y** is an example of a fingerspelled acronym (for "Teletypewriter"). Another example is **D-A** (for the *Deaf American*) which occurred in Unit 2.
>
> The sign **YOUR** ←→**POSS-*rt*** was discussed in the *General Discussion* section above. In this case, Pat is referring to Lee (**YOUR**) and Lee's new TTY which is on a table to Pat's right (**POSS-*rt***).
>
> Notice also that the sentence is a 'yes-no' question.

Lee₁:
nodding _____ cs
      NEW, RECENT ARRIVE-*here*

- nodding

   Notice that Lee responds to Pat's 'yes-no' question affirmatively by nodding.

_____ cs
- **RECENT ARRIVE**-*here*

   Notice that Lee uses the non-manual '*cs*' signal to indicate closeness to present time. Units 11 and 20 provide a description of this signal.
   Notice that the sign **ARRIVE**-___ can indicate the place of arrival by being signed in a specific location. See Units 4, 13, and 22 for more information on verbs of this type.

Pat₂:
nodding _____ (gaze rt _____) (nodding)q
      FINISH *you*-**TTY-CALL-TO**-*rt* *you*-**INFORM**-*rt* △, **FINISH** **YOU**
YOU

- *you*-**TTY-CALL-TO**-*rt* *you*-**INFORM**-*rt*

   These are examples of verbs which indicate their subject and/or object by their direction of movement. Units 4, 13, and 22 provide more information on verbs of this type. Notice how these verbs assign the location on the right to △ .

- △

   This is an example of a name sign in ASL. Name signs are generally given to a person by members of the Deaf Community. Some are based on a physical attribute of the person and some incorporate the initial letters of a person's first or last name. In some cases, Deaf parents will use the same location (e.g. over the heart; on the wrist) for the name signs of all their children but will vary the handshape to correspond to the child's "English" name.

Lee₂:
_____ t _____ wh-q
INFORM-*lf* △, **FOR-FOR**
        "WHAT"

- **INFORM**-*lf*

   Notice that Lee uses the location just assigned to △ — i.e. Pat's right. This is an example of how Signers in a conversation are consistent in the way they use locations for previously established referents.

<u>   wh-q   </u>

- **FOR-FOR** *"WHAT"*

    This is an example of a 'wh-word' question, as indicated by the non-manual signal. Notice that the gesture *"WHAT"* is made with only one hand—the non-dominant hand.

Pat$_3$:
  <u>   (gaze rt   )cond</u>   <u>   q</u>

SUPPOSE T-T-Y BREAK-DOWN, YOURSELF FIX QMwg

<u>   (gaze rt   )cond</u>

- **SUPPOSE T-T-Y BREAK-DOWN,**

    This is an example of the *condition* portion of a conditional question in ASL. Notice that the Signer uses the sign **SUPPOSE** in addition to the non-manual *'cond'* signal. See Units 10 and 19 for a discussion of conditionals.

    Notice also that Pat gazes to the right (the location of the **T-T-Y**) while signing **T-T-Y BREAK-DOWN.** This is an example of how head, eye, or body movements often accompany references to persons, places, or things.

<u>   q</u>

- **YOURSELF-FIX-QM**wg

    This is an example of the *comment* portion of a conditional question. The sign **YOURSELF** is a reflexive/emphatic pronoun. See Units 3 and 12 for a discussion of this type of pronoun.

    Notice that Pat ends the question with the sign **QMwg**. Often this sign is used to convey the meanings 'Really?!' or 'You gotta be kidding!'. There are two forms of this sign—**QMwg** and **QM.** The sign **QMwg** is more commonly used than the sign **QM**—which seems to be used in more formal situations.

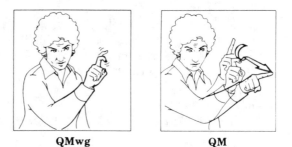

QMwg   QM

Lee₃: SILLY⌢ YOU,

       ME *me*-**SUMMON**-*rt*   **SOMEONE**-*rt*   (2h)**FROM**-*rt*-**COME-TO**-*here*   (2h)**#FIX***   (2h)**"WELL"**

- **SILLY⌢ YOU**

  This is an example of two signs which act as a single unit. Notice that the sign **SILLY*** is stressed by giving it a faster, tense 'flicking' of the wrist.

- *me*-**SUMMON**-*rt*   **SOMEONE**-*rt*   (2h)**FROM**-*rt*-**COME-TO**-*here*

  Notice that Lee uses a directional verb (____-**SUMMON**-____) to initially establish the location of the direct object to the right. The next sign (**SOMEONE**-*rt*) is made in that location to indicate who/what is the object. Finally, the next directional verb moves from that location toward the Signer, indicating that 'someone' is the subject of the verb.

- (2h)**# FIX***

  Notice that the fingerspelled loan sign **# FIX*** is signed with two hands and is also stressed.

                       _____t_____   _____nodding_____

Pat₄: △   **INDEX**-*rt,*   **FIX+**   **SKILL***   **POSS+** -*rt*
      "UMMM"

                             _____nodding_____

- **SKILL***   **POSS+** -*rt*

  Notice that the sign **SKILL** is stressed. What follows is an example of the possessive pronoun used to mean 'characteristic of' as described in the *General Discussion* section above. Notice the *'nodding'* signal which occurs at the end to emphasize that the statement is true.

                                                  q

Lee₄: **YOUR** **T-T-Y** **#FIX** **FINISH** **INDEX**-*lf* **QMwg**
      OH-I-SEE

- **INDEX**-*lf*

  Notice that Lee uses the spatial location which Pat has assigned to △ . This is another example of how Signers in a conversation are consistent in their use of space and in their references to previously established referents.

      _____nodding_____   _____nodding_____

Pat₅: **FAST** **WORK** **REALLY-ADEPT** **INDEX**-*rt*

- nodding

  The two instances of *'nodding'* in this turn serve different functions. The first instance is an affirmative response to Lee's 'yes-no' question (Lee₄). The second instance emphasizes that Pat's statement (**FAST   WORK   REALLY-ADEPT   INDEX**-*rt*) is true.

$$\text{Lee}_5:$$

$$\overline{}^{\text{nodding}}$$

ONE-DAY-FUTURE   ME   *me*-TTY-CALL-TO-*lf*

OH-I-SEE   FINE,

- *me*-T-T-Y-CALL-TO-*lf*

  Again notice that Lee is consistent in using the spatial location previously assigned to 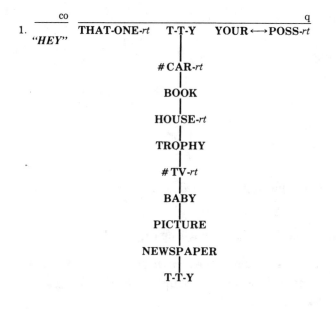 .

  Notice also the *'nodding'* which occurs throughout the sentence to emphasize the truth of the statement.

H. Sample Drills

1. $\overline{\text{THAT-ONE-}rt}^{\text{co}}$
"HEY"

THAT-ONE-*rt*   T-T-Y $\overline{\text{YOUR}\longleftrightarrow\text{POSS-}rt}^{\text{q}}$

|
#CAR-*rt*
|
BOOK
|
HOUSE-*rt*
|
TROPHY
|
#TV-*rt*
|
BABY
|
PICTURE
|
NEWSPAPER
|
T-T-Y

2. $\overline{\text{nodding}}$ $\overline{\text{FAST   WORK,}}^{\text{t}}$ 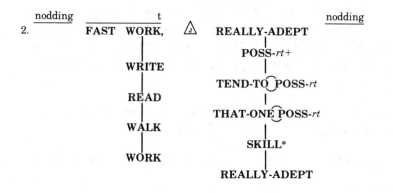   REALLY-ADEPT $\overline{}^{\text{nodding}}$

FAST   WORK,   REALLY-ADEPT
| |
WRITE   POSS-*rt*+
| |
READ   TEND-TO⌒POSS-*rt*
| |
WALK   THAT-ONE⌒POSS-*rt*
| |
WORK   SKILL*
                     |
              REALLY-ADEPT

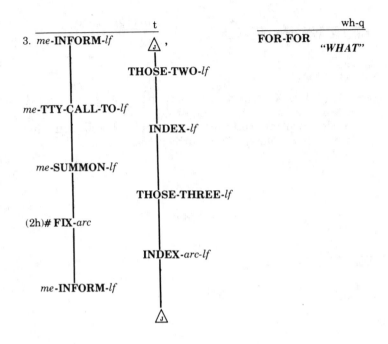

I. Video Notes

If you have access to the videotape package designed to accompany these texts, you will notice the following:

- The TTY next to Lee is a portable, "soft copy" machine called a Portatel.

- The non-manual behaviors which accompany the stressed signs **SILLY*⁀YOU** (Lee₃) and **SKILL*** (Pat₄). These include a brow squint, eye squint, and a sharp tilt of the head to one side and back.

- The *condition* portion of the conditional question in Pat₄ does not have the usual brow raise. Instead, the Signer tilts his head backward with his brows somewhat drawn together during the sign **SUPPOSE**. However, after the condition, he does shift his head and body position forward with a brow raise to signal that the *comment* is a 'yes-no' question.

- Pat seems to have a preference for the sign **FIX** (Pat₃ and ₄) whereas Lee seems to prefer the fingerspelled loan sign **# FIX** (Lee₃ and ₄).

- The repetition of **POSS**-*rt* in Pat₄ is so fast and small that it is almost imperceptible.

Unit 22

Subjects and Objects

A. Synopsis

Pat approaches Lee outside their office and asks why s/he looks so sad. Lee's uncle has died and Lee's mother is really depressed. It seems that Lee's mother and her brother didn't get along—they had been fighting for years. But now Lee is perplexed to see that his/her mother is really shaken up. Lee's mother got the insurance money from the FRAT yesterday after a couple of weeks of corresponding with them. But when she received the money, she burst into tears. She feels awful about hating her brother and now taking the money.

B. Cultural Information: The Fraternal Society of the Deaf (FRAT)

In 1901 at a Michigan School for the Deaf alumni reunion, an idea took hold that led to the establishment of the Fraternal Society of the Deaf during that same year in Chicago, Illinois. At that time, deaf individuals were discriminated against by insurance companies that made them pay higher premiums than were paid by hearing people. Thus, this group of deaf individuals worked out a way to provide for their own insurance by establishing their own organization—the National Fraternal Society of the Deaf (NFSD or the "FRAT"). Initially, membership in the FRAT was limited to adult males only, who paid $5.00 per week for sickness and accident benefits.

In 1904, the organization began its own official publication—a magazine called *The Frat*. By 1929, membership had grown to 6800 and by the end of the Depression years, its treasury had approximately two million dollars. In 1936, the FRAT remodeled a building which it owned and had its first fully-owned Home Office in Oak Park, a suburb of Chicago. In 1955, a new Home Office was built in Oak Park and housed the Home Office until 1975 when the FRAT moved to Mt. Prospect, Illinois.

Today the FRAT has over 13,000 members, seven million dollars in assets, and over 17 million dollars worth of insurance in force. Women now make up 35% of the total membership since they were permitted to join in 1951. There are more than 100 trained field representatives in the FRAT who are qualified to sell insurance. For more information, write: NFSD, 1300 W. Northwest Highway, Mt. Prospect, Ill. 60056.

C. Dialogue

Pat

$$\overline{\rule{2cm}{0pt}}^{\text{co}} \qquad\qquad\qquad \overline{\rule{3cm}{0pt}}^{\text{wh-q}}$$

Pat₁: "HEY", (2h)WHAT'S-UP SAD, (2h)WHAT'S-UP

Pat₂: *me-PITY-you*, $\overline{UNCLE\quad OLD}^{\text{q}}$

Pat₃: $\overline{UNCLE\quad DIE,}^{\text{t}}$ $\overline{HAVE\quad INSURANCE}^{\text{q}}$

Pat₄: $\overline{DIE,}^{\text{t}}$ MONEY $\overline{\text{C-CL-}lf\!\rightarrow\!rt\text{'take money from Frat'}}^{\text{(gaze lf}\qquad\qquad\qquad\text{)}}$ $\xrightarrow{\text{wh-q}}$
                                                                              "WHAT"

Pat₅: TOUCHING "WOW", TOUCHING "WOW"

Lee

Lee₁:
```
                          ____t____ (head tilt rt        )q
PAST ONE-MONTH UNCLE, MOTHER BROTHER, DIE, MOTHER BREAK-DOWN*
```

Lee₂:
```
     neg                      _____puff.cheeks_____  _____rhet.q
     AGE-FIFTY SIXTY THEREABOUTS, MOTHER DEPRESSED REASON
```

```
(gaze rt                                    )puff.cheeks
THOSE-TWO-rt  they-CLASH-WITH-"each other"+"regularly"  MANY*⌢YEAR  UP-TILL-NOW,
```

```
(gaze rt        )nodding  _____t_____ _____neg
SEEM  they-HATE-"each other",  (2h)NOW  MOTHER  BAWL-EYES-OUT,  ME  UNDERSTAND  ME
```

Lee₃:
```
____nodding____  _____q_____
FINISH++,  KNOW+  F-R-A-T,  UNCLE  JOHN-rt  LONG-TIME-PAST  NINETEEN  FIVE  ONE
```

Lee₄:
```
(gaze rt          )      (gaze rt                )
MOTHER TTY-CALL-TO-frat, INFORM-frat UNCLE DIE,
```

```
(gaze rt,cntr; body shift rt      ) (gaze rt                                    )
INDEX-rt    frat-SAY-#OK-TO-mother, TWO-FULL-WEEK they-CORRESPOND-WITH-"each other",
```

```
           ___cs+t___ (gaze rt      )
ONE-DAY-PAST, MONEY-rt frat-GIVE-TO-mother,
```

```
(gaze rt, look at money 'anguished'    )
MOTHER                              BAWL-EYES-OUT
        C-CL-rt→lf'take money from Frat',
```

Lee₅:
```
                    (gaze rt        )
MOTHER  CONSCIENCE, (2h)HATE-rt UNCLE,
```

```
(look at money'anguished'                                      )
TAKE-pile of money-FROM-frat MONEY PILE-OF-money, BAWL-EYES-OUT-rt CONSCIENCE++++
```

D. Key Illustrations

Pat

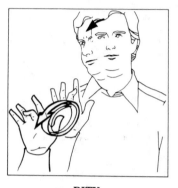

me-**PITY**-*you*

C-CL- *lf→rt* ——————→
"*WHAT*"

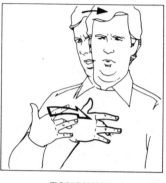

TOUCHING

Lee

THEREABOUTS

DEPRESSED

they-**CLASH-WITH-**
"*each other*"+"*regularly*"

MANY* YEAR

they-**HATE-**"*each other*"

BAWL-EYES-OUT

neg
UNDERSTAND

FINISH++

LONG-TIME-PAST

TTY-CALL-TO-*frat*

they-CORRESPOND-WITH-*"each other"*

CONSCIENCE+

E. Supplementary Illustrations

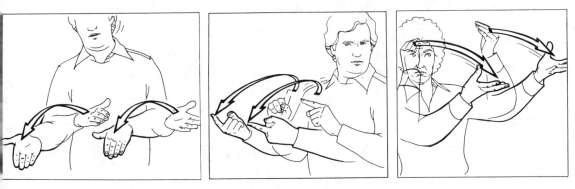

DIE

UP-TILL-NOW

INFORM-*lf*

F. General Discussion: Subjects and Objects

The two previous units on Subjects and Objects (Units 4 and 13) described how certain verbs make use of the space *around* the Signer's body (or a location *on* the Signer's body) to indicate the subject and/or object. Unit 13 also introduced the reader to reciprocal verbs and direct address. This unit will expand on some of the information in Units 4 and 13 and will show how differences in the handshape, movement, and/or size of a verb can identify the object.

By this point the reader should be quite comfortable with the fact that certain verbs in ASL use the actual or assigned locations of persons, places, or things to indicate their subject and/or object. Unit 13 provided a partial list of those *directional verbs* which appear in the student texts. The following verbs can be added to that list. (Most of these verbs are not contained in the student texts.)

——-ADVISE-——	——-INVITE-——
——-APPROACH-——	——-KISS-——
——-BEAT-——	——-MESH-WITH-——
——-BEAT-UP-——	——-ORDER/COMMAND-——
——-CHALLENGE-——	——-OVERCOME/DEFEAT-——
——-CONFRONT-——	——-PICK/SELECT-——
——-COPY-——	——-PICK-ON-——
——-DECEIVE/FOOL-——	——-PREACH-TO-——
——-FINGERSPELL-TO-——	——-SELL-TO-——
——-FINGERSPELL-NAME-TO-——	——-SHOOT-AT-——
——-FORCE-——	——-SHOW-TO-——
——-GET-EVEN-WITH-——	——-TEASE-——
——-GET-REVENGE-ON-——	——-TELL-TO-——
——-GIVE-ATTENTION-TO-——	——-TOUCH-——
——-HIT-——	——-USE-BIG-WORDS-TO-——

When a Signer makes a verb *reciprocal*, s/he is indicating that two people or two groups do the same thing to each other. Thus, by using two hands (each hand representing the action of one person or group), the Signer can indicate, for example, that two people 'hate each other' or 'look at each other', as illustrated below.

they-HATE-*"each other"*

they-LOOK-AT-*"each other"*

The following is a list of directional verbs which are or can be made *reciprocal* and which appear in the student texts.

____-AGREE-WITH-___	____-LOOK-AT-___
____-CLASH-WITH-___	____-MAKE-FUN-OF-___
____-CORRESPOND-WITH-___	____-PITY-___
____-DISCUSS-WITH-___	____-SAY-#NO-TO-___
____-GIVE-TO-___	____-SAY-#OK-TO-___
____-HATE-___	____-SAY-#YES-TO-___
____-INFORM-___	____-STRUGGLE-WITH-___
____-INSULT-___	____-TEACH-___

The verbs listed so far generally describe the action of one person or group (indicated by movement of the verb *from* a particular location) toward another person or group (indicated by movement of the verb *toward* a particular location). However, there are some verbs in ASL which indicate movement from one geographic location to another. This has been seen in verbs such as ____-GO-TO-___, ____-ARRIVE-AT-___, ____-FLY-TO-___, and ____-ENTER-___. The following is a partial list of directional verbs which can indicate movement from and/or to a specific geographic location. (This list does not include many of the ways that classifiers can be used as verbs to show movement from one location to another.)

> ____-ARRIVE-AT-___
> ____-ASSEMBLE-TO-___
> ____-BRING/CARRY-TO-___
> ____-COME/GO-TO
> COMMUTE-BETWEEN-___ & ___
> ____-DRIVE-TO-___
> ____-ENTER/GO-INTO-___
> ____-FLY-TO-___
> ____-JUMP-TO-___
> ____-MOVE-TO-___

Directional verbs are a clear example of how Signers use the space around their bodies for grammatical purposes. Similarly, verbs like **SHAVE-___** and **HAVE-OPERATION-ON-___** (described in Units 4 and 13) use locations on the Signer's body to indicate where various actions occur. In fact, this type of *location agreement* is the norm in ASL; when signs can be moved in space to 'agree', they usually are.

The example below illustrates this general fact about ASL.

```
        _____(gaze rt   )_____        t   (gaze rt                      )
(1)     L-E-E   POSS-rt   D-E-S-K,   CLEAN+ -rt   PERFECT*-rt,

        _____(gaze lf          )t   (gaze lf      )
        TABLE-lf   FOULED-UP-lf,   LEAVE-IT-lf
```

Translation: 'Lee cleaned up his desk really well, but didn't touch that messy table.'

In the example above, notice how the signs **POSS-*rt*,** **CLEAN-*rt*,** and **PERFECT-*rt*,** all 'agree' in location. Similarly, the signs **TABLE-*lf*,** **FOULED-UP-*lf*,** and **LEAVE-IT-*lf*** 'agree' in location. This type of *location agreement* is very common.

However, there are other ways that signs can 'agree with' each other. For example, many verbs will change their handshape to agree with the object of the verb. Some of these verbs are **PICK-UP-____** (e.g. marble, cup, rock), **POUR-FROM-____** (e.g. tea cup, pitcher, barrel), **THROW-____** (e.g. baseball, football, shotput), **BREAK-____** (e.g. twig, thick rod), **LIFT-____** (e.g. rock, suitcase), and **TAKE-____** (e.g. ball, box, bag). The choice of appropriate handshape in these verbs is usually determined by the size and shape (or some other physical characteristic) of the object that is 'thrown', 'broken', 'lifted', etc. Notice how the handshape of the verb **PICK-UP-____** agrees with the object in the illustrations below.

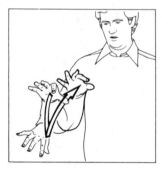
PICK-UP-____
(e.g. marble)

PICK-UP-____
(e.g. cup)

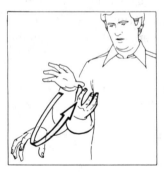
PICK-UP-____
(e.g. rock)

While these verbs give information about their object by a change in handshape, the sign **DRIVE-**___ uses a different type and size of movement to 'agree with' its object. Examine the different types and sizes of movements (as well as facial expressions) in the illustrations below.

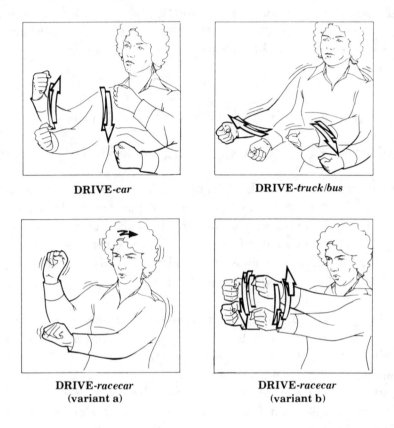

DRIVE-*car*   DRIVE-*truck/bus*

DRIVE-*racecar*   DRIVE-*racecar*
(variant a)   (variant b)

However, many verbs in ASL cannot be modulated to indicate or agree with their subject and/or object. Within this group, many are *body-anchored*—i.e. the production of the verb requires contact with the body. This body contact tends to limit the movability of the verb. The following is a partial list of verbs which generally do not indicate their subject and/or object and which appear in the student texts. (Some are not body-anchored.)

ACT/DRAMA	**KNOW**
BE-FED-UP	**LAUGH**
COMPLAIN	**LIVE**
DISOBEY/REBEL	**NOT-CARE**
DESIRE/WISH	**NOT-KNOW**
ENJOY	**THINK**
GUESS	**UNDERSTAND**
IMPROVE	**WALK**

When verbs like these are used in sentences, the Signer usually needs to sign the subject and/or object nouns—or use pronouns which indicate who or what is the subject and/or object—since the verb itself cannot convey that information. For example, notice the difference between the two conditional commands below. In the first conditional, the directional verb ____-FORCE-____ is modulated to show its subject and object. However, the verb **PUNISH** in the second conditional is body-anchored and cannot indicate its subject and object. So the Signer uses separate pronouns for these.

	(gaze lf) (	neg)	cond	tight lips
(2) **SUPPOSE**	**P-A-T-**_lf_ **NOT-WANT**		**WORK,**	_you_-**FORCE**-pat*

	(gaze lf) (	neg)	cond	tight lips
(3) **SUPPOSE**	**P-A-T-**_lf_ **NOT-WANT**		**WORK,**	**YOU PUNISH*** **INDEX-**_pat_

However, there is a rule in ASL which helps to reduce the need to continually re-state the subject of non-directional verbs. This rule has been called _the rule of last-mentioned subject_. This means that if several non-directional verbs (e.g. **WALK, ENJOY, LAUGH**) follow a subject noun, then that noun will be understood as the subject of all those verbs unless otherwise indicated. Thus if a Signer says **ONE-DAY-PAST** △ **WALK, ENJOY, LAUGH,** then △ is clearly the subject of all three verbs.

Sometimes _sign order_ (the actual order of the signs) and _topicalization_ can be used to clarify who or what is the subject and/or object when the verb is non-directional. For example, in the sentence that means 'Lee really loves Pat', if neither of the nouns are topicalized (signed first with the _'t'_ signal), then the sign order will be Subject-Verb-Object, as seen below. (Notice how the direction of the Signer's gaze during the verb **LOVE** also helps to show who is doing the loving—i.e. who is the subject.) When the Addressee sees a sentence like this with the order Noun-Verb-Noun, s/he will know that the first noun is the subject of the sentence.

	(gaze rt)(gaze lf) nodding
(4) **L-E-E-**_rt_	**LOVE P-A-T-**_lf_

Translation: 'Lee loves Pat.'

However, even when the verb is non-directional, the order of signs does not have to be Noun-Verb-Noun. For example, the object in the sentence can be topicalized. That is, the object noun can occur first in the sentence with the grammatical signal that shows it is a 'topic', as seen below. Here the order is Noun-Noun-Verb (Object-Subject-Verb). (Again, notice how the Signer gazes to the left—Pat's location— during the sign **LOVE**.)

	(gaze lf)t	(gaze rt)	(body lean rt, gaze lf)nodding
(5)	**P-A-T-**_lf_,	**L-E-E-**_rt_	**LOVE**

Translation: 'Lee loves Pat.' or 'Pat, Lee loves him.'

However, if the order is Noun-Verb-Noun and the first noun is topicalized, then the Addressee will understand that the first noun is the *subject* (not the object) in the sentence.

(6)
   (gaze lf)t (gaze rt) nodding
 P-A-T-*lf*, **LOVE L-E-E**-*rt*

  Translation: 'Pat loves Lee.'

In summary, if a verb is made in such a way that it can indicate its subject and/or object, there is a strong tendency in ASL to take advantage of the verb's "movability". However, not all verbs can be modulated to indicate their subject and/or object. These verbs are often body-anchored and, thus, have limited movability. In such cases, ASL Signers will use sign order and/or topicalization to indicate the subject or object—or use other devices like body shifting and gaze shifting, as described in Unit 13.

G. Text Analysis

      co   wh-q
Pat₁: "HEY", (2h)WHAT'S-UP SAD, (2h)WHAT'S-UP

> Notice that after getting Lee's attention with the gesture **"HEY"**, Pat asks a 'wh-word' question. The non-manual behaviors used to signal 'wh-word' questions are described in Units 1, 10, and 19.

         t (head tilt rt   )q
Lee₁: PAST ONE-MONTH UNCLE, MOTHER BROTHER, DIE, MOTHER BREAK-DOWN*

> • **PAST ONE-MONTH**
>
> Unlike the sign **ONE-WEEK**, the sign **ONE-MONTH** generally is not moved 'toward the past' or 'toward the future' to indicate past or future time. Thus, the Signer begins with the separate sign **PAST**.

       t (head tilt rt   )q
> • **UNCLE, MOTHER BROTHER**
>
> Notice that the sign **UNCLE** is the topic of the sentence. However, the Signer checks to see if the Addressee is familiar with the topic by providing clarifying information in the form of a 'yes-no' question. This is similar to what occurs in English when the Speaker says "My uncle—you know my mother's brother?—died yesterday". See the *General Discussion* section in Unit 19 for more explanation of this type of topic.

> • **BREAK-DOWN***
>
> Notice that this sign is stressed. The opposite of this sign is produced with an upward movement and conveys the meanings 'set up', 'establish', etc.

Pat_2: me-**PITY**-you, $\overline{UNCLE\quad OLD}^{\,q}$

- me-**PITY**-you

  This is a directional verb which indicates its subject and object by the direction of movement.

Lee_2: $\overline{\text{AGE-FIFTY}}^{\,neg}$ SIXTY $\overline{\text{THEREABOUTS,}}^{\,puff.cheeks}$ MOTHER DEPRESSED $\overline{\text{REASON,}}^{\,rhet.q}$

$\overline{\text{THOSE-TWO-}rt}^{(gaze\,rt}$ they-**CLASH-WITH**-"each other"+"regularly"$^{)puff.cheeks}$ MANY*⌒YEAR UP-TILL-NOW,

$\overline{\text{SEEM}}^{(gaze\,rt}$ they-**HATE**-"each other",$^{)nodding}$ $\overline{\text{(2h)NOW MOTHER BAWL-EYES-OUT,}}^{\,t}$ ME UNDERSTAND $\overline{\text{ME}}^{\,neg}$

- $\overline{\text{AGE-FIFTY}}^{\,neg}$ SIXTY $\overline{\text{THEREABOUTS}}^{\,puff.cheeks}$

  Notice that Pat responds to Lee's 'yes-no' question with the non-manual 'neg' signal. After responding, Pat then supplies more specific information about the uncle's age.

  The sign **AGE-FIFTY** is made by using the sign **FIVE**, touching the chin with the index finger and then moving the sign back and forth (usually twice) using the same wrist movement as for the sign **WHERE**. ASL Signers often use this back-and-forth wrist movement with number signs to express the meanings 'thirty', 'forty', 'fifty', 'sixty', etc. In fact, this is how the sign **SIXTY** is produced here. This is different than using the signs **SIX ZERO** to express the meaning 'sixty'.

  Notice that the Signer used the sign **THEREABOUTS** to indicate that 'fifty-sixty' is an approximation.

- **MOTHER DEPRESSED $\overline{\text{REASON}}^{\,rhet.q}$**

  This is a rhetorical question—not a true question, but a way for the Signer to introduce new information or a new topic of discussion. Notice that the sign **REASON** here has a meaning similar to the signs **WHY** or **WHYwg**.

- **$\overline{\text{THOSE-TWO-}rt}^{(gaze\,rt}$ they-CLASH-WITH-"each other"+"regularly"$^{)puff.cheeks}$**

  Since the Signer has not previously assigned a spatial location to **MOTHER** or **UNCLE**, the sign **THOSE-TWO-**rt gives them a location to the right. The sign ____-**CLASH-WITH-**____ is a directional verb which can be made reciprocal. Since both hands move toward each other (rather than only one hand move toward the other), it is clear that both 'mother' and 'uncle' are subjects of the verb. In addition, the Signer uses a modulation to indicate that the action occurred "regularly" (see Units 8, 17, and 26 for further information). Finally, notice that the Signer uses the *'puff.cheeks'* signal to indicate that the action happened 'a lot' or 'many times'.

<u>(gaze rt   )nodding</u>
- **SEEM** *they-***HATE-***"each other"*

  The sign ____-**HATE**-____ is another example of a directional verb which can be reciprocal. Notice in the illustration that each hand indicates the action/feeling of one person toward the other. When both hands perform the verb simultaneously, it shows that the two people do the same thing to each other. Each person is both a subject and object of the verb.

  Notice also that the Signer uses *'nodding'* to assert that the statement is true.

<u>   neg</u>
- **ME   UNDERSTAND   ME**

  Notice that the Signer does not use a manual sign (e.g. **NOT, DON'T**) to indicate negation. Instead, this information is conveyed solely by the non-manual *'neg'* signal.

Pat_4: <u> t </u>   <u>(gaze lf   )</u>   <u>wh-q</u>
        DIE,   MONEY   C-CL-*lf→rt*'take money from Frat' ——————→
                                           "WHAT"

- **C-CL-***lf→rt*'take money from Frat'

  This classifier is often used by ASL Signers to refer to 'a chunk of money' or 'an unknown sum of money' and frequently occurs when discussing investments, deposits, withdrawals, etc.

Lee_4: **(gaze rt   )   (gaze rt   )**
      MOTHER TTY-CALL-TO-*frat*, **INFORM-***frat* **UNCLE DIE,**

(gaze rt,cntr; body shift rt   )   (gaze rt   )
    INDEX-*rt*   *frat*-**SAY-#OK-TO-***mother*, **TWO-FULL-WEEK** *they-***CORRESPOND-WITH-***"each other"*,

<u>   cs+t</u> **(gaze rt   )**
    ONE-DAY-PAST, MONEY-*rt* *frat*-**GIVE-TO-***mother*,

(gaze rt; look at money 'anguished'   )
    MOTHER   **BAWL-EYES-OUT**
        C-CL-rt→lf'take money from Frat',

- **TTY-CALL-TO-***frat*

  This is another example of a directional verb which can indicate its subject and/or object by the direction of movement. In this case, since Lee has previously established the Frat to the right (in Lee_3-... **UNCLE JOIN-***rt* ...) the direction of movement is toward the right. But the verb moves toward a location farther away on the right to distinguish the location of the 'Frat' from that of the 'mother' and 'uncle'.

(body shift rt   )
- *frat*-**SAY-# OK-TO**-*mother,*

> This is an example of a fingerspelled loan sign **# OK** which
> is used as a directional verb. Other loan signs which can
> be used as directional verbs include **# NO, # YES,** and
> **# BACK.**
>
> Notice also that the Signer's body shifts to the right—
> the location assigned to the Frat. This is an example of
> how Signers will often "role play" when quoting someone
> (i.e. in direct address). Since the 'mother' is also located to
> the right (but closer to the Signer than the 'Frat'), the verb
> moves from a location further away on the right (repre-
> senting the 'Frat') to a location closer to Lee on the right
> (representing the 'mother').

(gaze rt   )
- **TWO-FULL-WEEK**   *they*-**CORRESPOND-WITH-**"*each other*"

> The sign **TWO-FULL-WEEK** is made by using a slow
> movement for the beginning portion of the sign and a
> faster movement for the final segment of the sign. Com-
> pare the following illustrations of the signs **TWO-WEEK**
> and **ONE-FULL-WEEK** and notice the differences in
> movement.

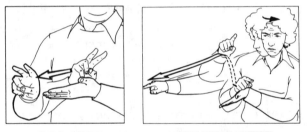

TWO-WEEK   **ONE-FULL-WEEK**

The sign ___-**CORRESPOND-WITH-**___ is an example of a directional verb that is always reciprocal.

<u>   cs+t   </u>
- **ONE-DAY-PAST**

> Notice that the Signer uses the *'cs'* signal (to indicate 'closeness in time') in addition to the non-manual signal for a topic. Examine the photo below to see what this combination of the *'cs'* and *'t'* signal looks like.

<u>   cs+t   </u>
MORNING

(gaze rt; look at money 'anguished')
- **MOTHER**   **BAWL-EYES-OUT**
       C-CL-*rt→lf* 'take money from **FRAT'**,

> Notice that here again Lee "role plays" the 'mother' so that the 'money' actually moves from the location of the 'Frat' to Lee (who has become the 'mother'). In the role of the 'mother', Lee looks at the money with anguish and then tells how the 'mother' responded (**BAWL-EYES-OUT**).

(gaze rt   )
Lee₅: **MOTHER CONSCIENCE,** (2h)**HATE**-*rt* **UNCLE,**

(look at money 'anguished'   )
TAKE-*pile of money*-**FROM**-*frat* **MONEY PILE-OF**-*money*, **BAWL-EYES-OUT**-*rt* **CONSCIENCE**+++

- (2h)**HATE**-*rt*

> Since the direction of both hands is toward the right (the location of the 'uncle'), the sign is not reciprocal as it was in Lee₂.

(look at money 'anguished'   )
- **TAKE**-*pile of money*-**FROM**-*frat* **MONEY PILE-OF**-*money*

> Notice that again Lee "role plays" and becomes the 'mother'. As described in the *General Discussion* section above, the verb **TAKE-FROM-____** 'agrees with' its object—here, a 'pile of money'. To take this pile of money, the 'mother' (Lee) uses both hands—one open hand holding the bottom of the pile and the other open hand holding the top.
>
> The sign glossed as **PILE-OF**-*money* is exactly like the preceding verb except that it does not have the movement 'take from'.

- **CONSCIENCE++++**

  This sign is often glossed as **GUILTY.** However, since it is used to express meanings like 'pangs of conscience' and 'rapid heartbeat' and since the gloss **GUILTY** has a negative connotation, it seems more appropriate to use the gloss **CONSCIENCE.**

H. Sample Drills

(gaze rt   )puff.cheeks

1. **THOSE-TWO**-*rt*   *they*-**CLASH-WITH**-"*each other*"+"*regularly*"   **MANY**⁎ **YEAR**   **UP-TIL-NOW**

        they-**CHALLENGE**-"*each other*"+"*regularly*"

        they-**CORRESPOND-WITH**-"*each other*"+"*regularly*"

        they-**STRUGGLE-WITH**-"*each other*"+"*regularly*"

        they-**GIVE-TO**-"*each other*"+"*regularly*"

        they-**MAKE-FUN-OF**-"*each other*"+"*regularly*"

        they-**PREACH-TO**-"*each other*"+"*regularly*"

        they-**DISAGREE-WITH**-"*each other*"+"*regularly*"

        they-**CLASH-WITH**-"*each other*"+"*regularly*"

(gaze rt, cntr; body shift rt   )   (gaze rt   )

2. **INDEX**-*rt*   *frat*-**SAY-#OK-TO**-*mother* ,   **TWO-FULL-WEEK**   *they*-**CORRESPOND-WITH**-"*each other*"

        frat-**SAY-#NO-TO**-*mother*

                                      they-**MAKE-FUN-OF**-"*each other*"

        frat-**SAY-#YES-TO**-*mother*

                                      they-**STRUGGLE-WITH**-"*each other*"

        frat-**TTY-CALL-TO**-*mother*

                                      they-**CORRESPOND-WITH**-"*each other*"

        frat-**SAY-#OK-TO**-*mother*

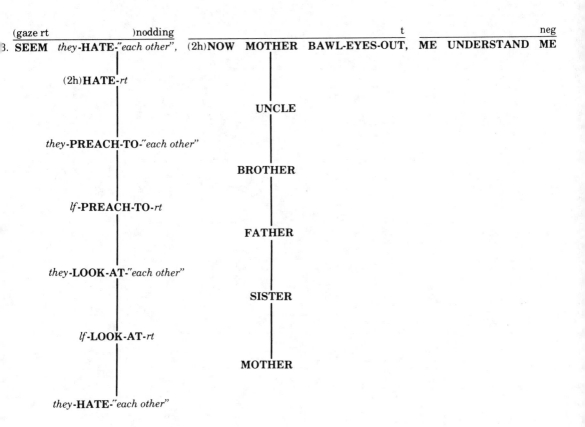

I. Video Notes

If you have access to the videotape package designed to accompany these texts, you will notice the following:

- Right before Pat's second turn and as she signs *me*-**PITY**-*you,* she uses a "facial sign" that involves an opening and closing of the mouth, with the upper teeth then pressing against the lower lip. This means 'that's awful' or 'that's terrible'.

- In Lee$_2$, the sign **MANY** is stressed, but not joined to the sign **YEAR** in the way illustrated above.

- In Lee$_3$, the sign **LONG-TIME-PAST** moves straight back over the shoulder rather than with a looping movement as illustrated above. These signs are variants with basically the same meaning.

- In Lee$_4$, he signs **ONE-DAY-PAST** with the pinky extended—a variant of the same sign with only the thumb extended. Also notice the combined 'cs' + 't' signals.

- In Lee$_5$, beginning with the sign **HATE**-*rt,* Lee's body turns to face the location of the 'uncle', clearly signaling that Lee has become the 'mother'. His body stays in this position for the rest of the turn.

Unit 23

Classifiers

A. Synopsis

Pat joins Lee during a coffee break and explains a dumb thing that happened the other day. It seems Pat was working and knocked his/her alarm clock off the desk and it broke and now s/he wants to get it fixed. Lee suggests asking Tina who owns a store and both sells and repairs alarms. Lee says that the store is located not far from a really fancy house that both Pat and Lee know. Pat says s/he will go to Tina's tomorrow.

B. Cultural Information: Alarms/Signaling Devices for Deaf People

It should not be surprising that many of the alarms and signaling devices that are used by hearing people are not effective for many deaf people since these alarms and devices generally rely on sound. As a result, special alarms and signaling devices are now commercially available which rely on vision or vibration to signal the user. Some of these signaling devices are listed below. This list is not intended to be complete, but merely represents the range of the kinds of devices that are now available to deaf people.

Vibrating Alarm Timer: a heavy-duty bed vibrator that is plugged into an electric timer which can be pre-set to vibrate the bed at a specific time.

Electro-Alarm Clock: a standard clock with a large lighted clock face which is attached to a small pillow vibrator that vibrates at any pre-set time.

Flash Alarm: a clock with an attached light which flashes on and off at any pre-set time.

Whisper Lights: specially built lamps (or attachments to lamps) which are sound-activated and can be used to detect a baby crying, a knock on the door, etc.

Telephone/Doorbell Signaler: lights which are attached to the doorbell and/or tele-phone so that they flash if someone pushes the doorbell or if the phone rings.

Smoke Detectors: these devices are also connected to lights or bed vibrators which are activated in case of a fire.

For more information about specific products, see advertisements in the *Deaf American,* the monthly magazine published by the National Association of the Deaf, 814 Thayer Avenue, Silver Spring, Md. 20910.

C. Dialogue

Pat

Pat₁:
                         co
      "HEY", ME PEA-BRAIN*, TRUE+ MAKE-ME-SICK*

Pat₂:
                               cs   br (gaze down)   (gaze down   )   t
      HAPPEN FEW-DAY-PAST, ME WORK, TABLE PAPER (2h)alt.B↓-CL'papers on table',

      (gaze down,rt   )t   (nodding   )q
      TIME A-CL@rt'clock', BURST-OF-*light-rt++* KNOW YOU

Pat₃:
                             (head,gaze lf   )
      ME+ CARELESS, "move arm to right suddenly"

      (gaze down,rt   )   wh-q
      A-CL'clock on table,fall off' (2h)SHATTER/SPLATTER-*rt* "SHUCKS", ME (2h)#DO-DO
      B↓-CL'table'

Pat₄:
      neg   (gaze down,rt   ) wh-q
      CHERISH, MOTHER *rt*-GIVE-TO-*me*, CHERISH*, WANT-*rt* (2h)#FIX-*rt*, HOWwg

Pat₅:
                         wh-q
      STORE WHERE "WHAT"

Pat₆:
                                            nodding
      ONE-DAY-FUTURE #WILL ME GO-TO-*store* #WILL

Lee

               wh-q   neg

ee₁: **#WHAT, NOT UNDERSTAND**

                                             nodding

ee₂: **RIGHT+, you-SAME-AS-*me* MY+ *you-SAME-AS-me***

                                     nodding

ee₃: **"SO-WHAT", (2h)IT'S-NOTHING, BUY-TO-*lf* NEW+**

        t   neg   neg   neg+q

ee₄: **ME, INEPT, WHY͡NOT you-ASK-TO-*rt* △,   KNOW T-I-N-A**

      nodding   puff.cheeks   nod   t

   INDEX-*rt*+ SKILL* FIX++-*arc* THUMB-INDEX-*rt*, POSS-*rt* STORE,

       nod   puff.cheeks

   HAVE+ TIME͡(2h)C-CL'clock' A-CL*"sweep in rows"*, REALLY-ADEPT INDEX-*rt*

                                    (gaze at'street'   )t

ee₅: **(2h)"WELL" KNOW+ FANCY HOME 5:↓-CL@*rt*'fancy home',** ⟶
                                                                      B-CL'street running next to fancy home',

        t   (gaze lf,cntr)   (gaze at 'home'&'store')

   STORE, INDEX-lf,cntr NOT-MUCH INDEX-home & store↔ ⟶

D. Key Illustrations

Pat

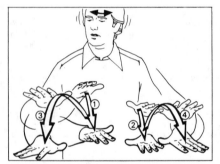

PEA-BRAIN*

MAKE-ME-SICK*

FEW-DAY-PAST

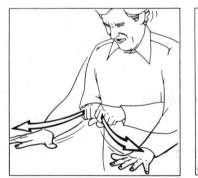

(2h)alt.B↓-CL'papers on table'

BURST-OF-light-*rt*++

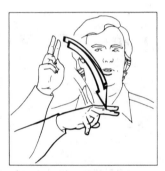

CARELESS

(2h)SHATTER/SPLATTER

CHERISH

HOWwg

Lee

#WHAT

(2h)IT'S-NOTHING

INEPT

A-CL"*sweep in rows*"

REALLY-ADEPT

5:↓-CL@rt '*fancy home*'

5:↓-CL-rt
B-CL'street'

5:↓-CL-rt
INDEX-lf,cntr

5:↓-CL-rt
NOT-MUCH

E. Supplementary Illustrations

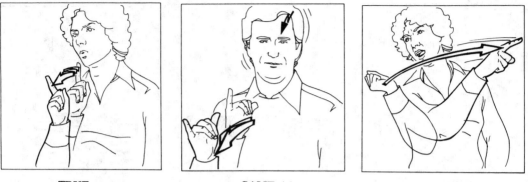

TRUE++   *you*-SAME-AS-*me*   *you*-ASK-TO-*lf*

F. General Discussion: Classifiers

The previous discussions of classifiers in Units 5 and 14 dealt with the various functions of classifiers—some acting as pronouns which can show the actions and locations of various referents (people, animals, things), and others acting more like adjectives which describe the size, shape, or texture of those referents. Unit 14 also touched on a few ways that the Signer's *perspective* can influence his/her choice of which classifier to use to represent something or describe it. This unit will describe in more depth what is meant by the Signer's *perspective* and how it influences the selection and use of classifiers.

The Signer's *perspective* includes both what s/he actually *sees* and what s/he chooses to *focus on* (within that 'mass' of things that s/he actually sees). Let's first consider what the Signer *sees*. For example, suppose there is a meeting in which a group of people are seated in a semi-circle around the speaker who is facing them. The Signer arrives late and stands at the back of the room. The Signer *sees* the backs of the people, and the people in the middle of the semi-circle are the ones closest to him/her.

(2h)4:-CL
'in semi-circle with backs to Signer'

However, suppose the Signer is the speaker at the meeting. Now the Signer *sees* the faces of the people, and the people in the middle of the semi-circle are the ones farthest away from him/her.

(2h)4:-CL
'in semi-circle facing Signer'

In that example, the Signer's *perspective* (what s/he actually saw) influenced the palm orientation of the classifier and the way the semi-circle was 'outlined'.

Now remember the example of the 'cattle' in Unit 14. On the ranch, there is a huge herd of cattle pleasantly milling around, searching for new patches of grass. That's what the Signer *sees*. However, when describing the ranch to a friend the next day, the Signer chooses to *focus on* the fact that there was a huge herd of cattle there but does not indicate what they were doing.

(2h)5:↓-CL
'huge herd of cattle'

The classifier used above does not indicate if the cattle were stationary or moving; it could be used in either case. But now suppose the Signer chooses to include that information when describing the cattle. Now the Signer chooses to also *focus on* the 'unorderly movement' in addition to the 'huge herd'. So the Signer uses the classifier with 'wiggly' finger movement (perhaps with both hands overlapping each other repeatedly).

(2h)5↓wg-CL
'herd of cattle milling around'

In that example above, both what the Signer *saw* and what s/he chose to *focus on* influenced the choice and use of the classifier.

The distance between the Signer and the thing s/he wants to describe can also determine the choice of classifier. Naturally, the closer the Signer is to the thing, the larger it appears and the more 'detail' s/he can see. For example, suppose the Signer sees a 'bin' far away that has something green inside it. From a distance, the green surface (the top) appears to be 'smooth'. So the Signer describes what s/he sees as:

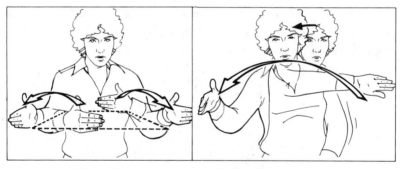

(2h)B-CL'bin'   **B↓-CL'smooth curved surface'**

Now suppose the Signer is standing close enough to see that the green stuff is not one solid mass but is composed of many different things of the same kind all thrown together. The surface now appears more 'uneven'; so the Signer uses a '5' handshape to describe this surface.

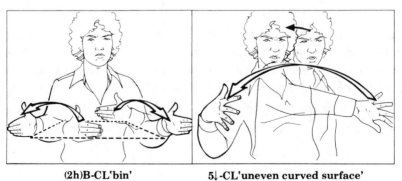

(2h)B-CL'bin'   **5↓-CL'uneven curved surface'**

Now when the Signer moves a little closer, s/he sees that the green things are ears of corn all thrown together in the bin. The Signer might describe this unorderly arrangement as follows:

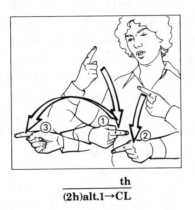

$$\overline{\text{th}}$$
(2h)alt.1→CL

Or, if the ears of corn were arranged neatly in ascending rows, the Signer might describe them as follows:

(2h)1→CL-*upward"sweep in a row"*

If the Signer then moves even closer to the bin so that the ears of corn become 'larger' visually, s/he may choose to use a different classifier to describe them. These ascending rows of corn could be described in either of the ways illustrated below.

(2h)C-CL-*upward"sweep in rows"*   (2h)C$_t$-CL-upward"sweep in rows"

Thus, we can see how distance can influence what the Signer *sees* and, therefore, can influence the Signer's selection and use of classifiers. However, again this selection and use also depends on what the Signer chooses to *focus on*. For example, the Signer could be standing right next to the bin of corn and still only describe it as a 'bin' with a 'pile of' corn inside, rather than specify exactly how the corn is arranged.

Let's look at another example. Suppose someone asks the Signer to describe the Capitol Building in Washington, D.C.—both from a distance far away and from a close-up perspective. From very far away, the Signer might use the '1' handshape (both hands) to outline the building and to indicate the location of the columns (which would simply appear as straight parallel lines). As the Signer moved a little closer, the columns would begin to have some width (indicated with the 'G' handshape). Or, the Signer might see that they are circular (indicated with the 'F' handshape).

'Columns seen from a distance'

'1' handshape
'parallel lines'

'G' handshape
'parallel lines with some width'

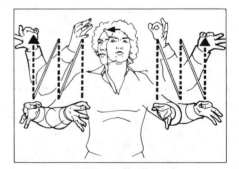

'F' handshape
'narrow parallel columns'

However, if the Signer is standing closer to the Capitol Building, the columns would appear much larger and have more depth. This could be described as shown below on the left. If the Signer stands very close to the building, the columns would look enormous and could be described as shown below on the right.

'Columns seen from close-up'

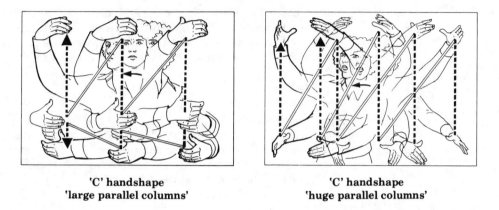

| 'C' handshape | 'C' handshape |
| 'large parallel columns' | 'huge parallel columns' |

Thus, in these examples, we see that the choice of classifier may be determined by the size and shape of the thing being described—but again, is mediated by the Signer's perception of that size and shape. From afar, things appear small and to have fewer dimensions. As the Signer moves closer, things appear larger and more three-dimensional (having height, width, and depth). However, as stated earlier, how something is described also depends on what the Signer wants to focus on. The Signer may choose to describe the columns of the Capitol building as 'huge parallel columns' or simply remark that there are 'parallel columns' in front of the building. Thus, the actual features of the referent (e.g. size, shape, texture), the Signer's perception of those features, and the Signer's choice of what to focus on all influence the appropriate choice of classifier handshapes.

G. Text Analysis

$$\text{Pat}_1: \quad \overset{co}{\text{"HEY"}}, \quad \text{ME} \quad \text{PEA-BRAIN*}, \quad \text{TRUE+} \quad \text{MAKE-ME-SICK*}$$

- **MAKE-ME-SICK***

    This sign is often directed toward a specific person, place, or thing (or the location assigned to it). When this occurs, the movement used is a thrusting outward motion and not the twisting motion illustrated above. It conveys the meanings 'that disgusts me', 'I'm sick of that', 'the hell with ____', 'who needs it?!', etc.

		cs		br	(gaze down)		(gaze down)		t

Pat₂: **HAPPEN FEW-DAY-PAST, ME WORK, TABLE PAPER** (2h)alt.**B↓-CL**'papers on table',

	(gaze down,rt)t		(nodding)q

  TIME A-CL@_rt_'clock',   **BURST-OF**-_light-rt++_   **KNOW YOU**

- (2h)alt.**B↓-CL**'papers on table'

  Notice that the Signer has clearly indicated what this classifier is representing by first signing **PAPER.** Also notice that Lee has used the two-hands alternating plural modulation to show that the papers are scattered all over the desk.

- **A-CL@**_rt_'clock'

  Again notice that the referent for this classifier is indicated with the preceding sign **TIME.** The particular classifier used (**A-CL**) makes it clear that the Signer means a clock and not a watch—since a different classifier (**F-CL**) would be used to represent a watch.

- **BURST-OF**-_light-rt++_

  This classifier occurred in an earlier dialogue (Unit 5) where it also represented a kind of light (stop light). However, it can also be used to refer to water (e.g. a shower) or sound (e.g. a trumpet blaring).

  (nodding   )q
- **KNOW   YOU**

  Notice that although Pat is checking to see whether Lee understands or not, Pat's nodding seems to indicate that s/he expects a positive response.

			nodding

Lee₂: **RIGHT+,** _you_-**SAME-AS**-_me_ **MY+** _you_-**SAME-AS**-_me_

- _you_-**SAME-AS**-_me_

  Notice that this sign moves from the Addressee (Pat) to the Signer (Lee). It functions in the same way as directional verbs. That is, it can move between two people, places, things or their spatial locations to indicate that they are 'just alike' or 'the same as each other'.

	(head,gaze lf)	

Pat₃: **ME+ CARELESS,** "move arm to right suddenly"

	(gaze down,rt		)	wh-q

A-CL'clock on table,fall off' (2h)**SHATTER/SPLATTER**-_rt_ **"SHUCKS", ME** (2h)**#DO-DO**
B↓-CL'table'

- **CARELESS**

  This sign can be made with one or two hands.

(head,gaze lf   )
- "move arm to right suddenly"

> Notice that Pat looks to the left while showing what hap-
> pened on the right. This indicates that Pat didn't see that
> his/her arm was moving toward the clock.

A-CL'clock on table, fall off'
- *B↓-CL'table'*

> Notice that the meaning of these two classifiers is clear
> from Pat's previous turn. Notice also how they provide
> locative information—the clock was *on the table* and then
> it fell *off*.

- (2h)**SHATTER/SPLATTER**

> This sign may, in fact, be a classifier for a sudden 'explo-
> sion' of parts or pieces (represented by the fingers) from a
> single source (represented by the closed hands). Notice the
> similarity between this sign and the sign **DISPERSE**
> illustrated below.

DISPERSE

nodding

Lee₃: **"SO-WHAT",** (2h)**IT'S-NOTHING, BUY-TO-***lf* **NEW +**

- (2h)**ITS-NOTHING**

> This sign can also be made with one hand. It expresses the
> meaning that someone or something is 'trivial', 'not worth
> getting upset about', or 'not a big deal'.

<pre>
          t   neg   ⌢   neg   neg+q
Lee₄: ME, INEPT, WHY NOT you-ASK-TO-rt   △ ,   KNOW T-I-N-A
</pre>

<pre>
        nodding   puff.cheeks   nod   t
     INDEX-rt+   SKILL* FIX++-arc THUMB-INDEX-rt, POSS-rt STORE,
</pre>

<pre>
        nod   ⌢   puff.cheeks
     HAVE+ TIME (2h)C-CL'clock' A-CL"sweep in rows", REALLY-ADEPT INDEX-rt
</pre>

- neg
  INEPT

  > Some Signers produce this sign with movement in the opposite direction—i.e. away from the Signer instead of toward the Signer.

- neg   neg+q
  KNOW   T-I-N-A

  > Lee's initial *'neg'* reaction is because Pat did not recognize the name sign △ . Lee then spells **T-I-N-A.** When Pat shakes his head to show that he doesn't know who Tina is, Lee responds *'neg+q'* (meaning 'you don't know her?'). Examine the photos showing the *'neg+q'* signal in the *General Discussion* section of Unit 19 to see what this combined signal looks like.

- puff.cheeks
  FIX++ -arc

  > Notice that the *'puff.cheeks'* and the *arc* movement serve to convey the fact that Tina is good at fixing 'many things'.

- **TIME (2h)C-CL'clock'**

  > Notice that these two signs are produced in such a way that they look like a single sign. The (2h)**C-CL** is often used when referring to a clock that hangs on a wall. Notice that this classifier gives more information about the shape of the clock (indicating that it is round) than the **A-CL** (Pat₂).

- puff.cheeks
  A-CL"sweep in rows"

  > Notice that both the *"sweep in rows"* modulation and the *"puff.cheeks"* signal convey the meanings 'many', 'a lot of', or 'a huge number of'. Also, in this context, the *"sweep in rows"* modulation suggests that the clocks are in rows on shelves.

```
                                                   (gaze at'street'                        )t
(2h)"WELL"  KNOW+  FANCY  HOME  5:↓-CL@rt'fancy home', ─────────────────────→
                                                   B-CL'street running next to fancy home',
```

```
              t   (gaze lf,cntr  )                 (gaze at 'home'&'store')
(hold 5:↓-CL)─────────────────────────────────────────→
             STORE,  INDEX-lf,cntr  NOT-MUCH  INDEX-home & store↔
```

```
                         (gaze at 'street'                     )
• 5:↓-CL@rt'fancy home'──────────────────────────→
                         B-CL'street running next to fancy home'
```

These two classifiers were used in a similar way in Unit 15. Notice how they indicate the locative relationship between the 'street' and the 'home'. Notice also that Lee holds the 5:↓-CL for the rest of his/her turn. This is because it will be used as a point of reference for the 'street' and 'Tina's store'.

• *NOT-MUCH*

This sign is often used when talking about distances ('not far') but can also refer to prices ('not expensive' or 'real cheap').

• *INDEX-home & store ↔*

Notice in the illustration that the back and fourth movement of the **INDEX** between the 'home' and the 'store' is small. Thus, this sign 'agrees with' the fact that the distance between them is **NOT-MUCH.**

```
                                  nodding
ONE-DAY-FUTURE  #WILL  ME  GO-TO-store  #WILL
```

• *#WILL*

This is a fingerspelled loan sign. Notice also that the 'nodding' is used to confirm Pat's stated intention that s/he will go to the store.

H. Sample Drills

<pre>
                 cs   br   t   (nodding   )q
1. FEW-DAY-PAST, ME   WORK, TABLE TIME A-CL@rt'clock', BURST-OF-light++, KNOW YOU
                                                   |
                                           A-CL@lf'clock'
                                                   |
                                          A-CL@cntr'clock'
                                                   |
                                      A-CL@rt'clock on table'
                                      B↓-CL-rt'table'
                                                   |
                                      A-CL@cntr'clock on table'
                                      B↓-CL-cntr'table'
                                                   |
                                      A-CL@lf'clock on table'
                                      B↓-CL-lf'table'
                                                   |
                                          A-CL@cntr'clock'
                                                   |
                                           A-CL@lf'clock'
                                                   |
                                           A-CL@rt'clock'
</pre>

<pre>
              t   nod   puff.cheeks
2. POSS-rt STORE,   HAVE+   TIME (2h)C-CL'clock'   A-CL"sweep in rows"

       HOME
                                                  (2h)alt.A-CL'clocks'

     MOTHER
                                                    A-CL"in a row"

     SCHOOL
                                                  A-CL"sweep in a row"

     SISTER
                                                    A-CL"in rows"

      STORE
                                                  A-CL"sweep in rows"
</pre>

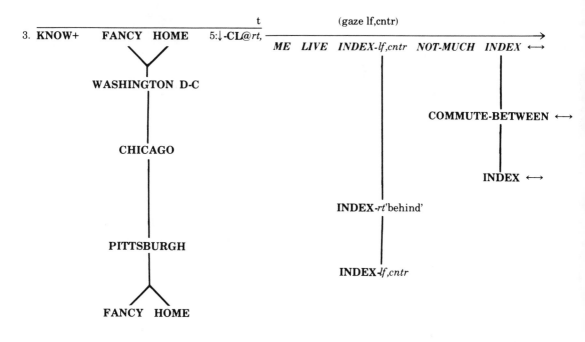

I. Video Notes

If you have access to the videotape package designed to accompany these texts, you will notice the following:

- In Pat$_2$, how he clearly indicates the relative locations of the table, scattered papers, and alarm clock by his consistent use of space and eye gaze.

- How Lee uses his left wrist as the place of contact for the sign **RIGHT** (Lee$_2$) because he is holding a cup in his left hand. When one hand is 'busy', Signers commonly use some other surface (e.g. chest, knee if seated, book if holding one, table) for signs that require contact.

- In Lee$_4$, how the 'neg' signal during the sign **INEPT** does not give the meaning 'not inept'. Instead, it's like saying two things at the same time—'No, I'm not the one to do it' ('neg'); I'm no good at that' (**INEPT**). Notice how this is different from the way the 'neg' signal in Lee$_1$ (or more obviously in Lee$_2$, Unit 22) does negate the verb **UNDERSTAND**, giving the meaning 'not understand'.

- In Lee$_5$, how he holds the 5:↓-**CL@**rt with his right hand as a reference point while clearly indicating the relative locations of the 'store' and the 'home'.

Unit 24

Locatives

A. Synopsis

Lee has just returned from a skiing trip. Pat asks what happened to Lee's eye. Lee explains that s/he was skiing down a hill which is next to a nearby farm when s/he swerved to avoid hitting a rabbit and then fell over a fence. S/he not only hurt his/her eye but also the left shoulder.

B. Cultural Information: World Games for the Deaf

In 1924, representatives from nine European countries met in Paris, France and established the International Committee of Silent Sports (CISS—"Comite International des Sports Silencieux"). This committee was developed to establish a union of all sports federations for deaf people and to institute and manage quadrennial World Games for the Deaf. The United States joined the CISS in 1935 as its first non-European nation. Until 1948, only Summer Games were held. Then in 1949, the first Winter Games were held in Seefeld, Austria. In 1955, the CISS was acknowledged by the International Olympic Committee as an international federation with Olympic standing. Currently, Jerald M. Jordan of the United States is President of the CISS and has served in that capacity since 1971.

The World Games for the Deaf are held exclusively for persons with a certain level of hearing loss, and each national federation is required to verify that its competitors do, in fact, have a hearing loss at or below this level. Those athletes with very mild losses are not permitted to compete. In fact, pretending to be deaf is considered as serious an offense as taking drugs in the "hearing Olympics".

The World Games features competition in such events as track and field, cycling, soccer, gymnastics, handball, wrestling, swimming, diving, ping-pong, skiing, tennis, shooting and volleyball.

C. Dialogue

Pat

Pat₁:
```
                                                  (                    puff.cheeks)wh-q
      (2h)"WHAT"  HAPPEN  INDEX-Lee's rt cheek  PURPLE 5:-CL'bruise on cheek'  YOU
```

Pat₂:
```
                                    wh-q
      (2h)"WHAT"  (2h)#DO-DO  (2h)"WHAT"
```

Pat₃:
```
      nodding  (gaze rt      )        (gaze rt        )                                      q
               THAT-ONE-rt  FARM   THEREABOUTS-rt ───────────────→THAT-ONE-rt  YOU
                                               B-CL-lf 'hillside' ─────────────────────→
```

Pat₄: WOW REALLY-ADEPT YOU

Pat₅:
```
                          nodding                              q
      "WOW"+,  #HURT  INDEX-cheek   OTHER+  (2h)"WHAT"
```

Lee

Lee₁: **FEW-DAY-PAST ME SKI BAD HAPPEN INDEX**-*lf cheek*

_____(gaze down,lf_____)_(gaze at 'hill'_____)_____q
Lee₂: **YOU KNOW WATER**◯**(2h)L:-CL**@*lf* 'lake' **B-CL**-*rt*'hillside next to lake', **KNOW YOU**
                           (hold lf hand L:-CL) ————————————————————————→

____nodding__(gaze down,cntr____)_____br
Lee₃: **RIGHT+, B-CL**-*cntr*'front face of hill', **ME V-CL**@*cntr*'stand on hilltop'
            B-CL-*cntr*'*hilltop*' ——————————————————→

(gaze lf at 'fence'_____)_(gaze rt_)_____br
(2h)4-CL-*lf*'fence on side of hill',   **TREE**-*rt,upward-arc*'trees on side of hill',

          (gaze down,cntr; look of'concentration'; body moving from side to side)
       ME   SKI   1-CL-*cntr*'ski down hillside,weaving side to side'

                                                           t
Lee₄: **"PSHAW", 1-CL**-*cntr*'ski down hillside', ‾R‾A‾B‾B‾I‾T‾,

                                        (look of 'fright'   )
       V:-CL-*rt*'hop from trees in front of me'   **ME   1-CL**'swerve to lf to miss rabbit'

   (gaze lf, 'shocked'   )
          (2h)4-CL-*lf*'fence' **V-CL**-*lf*'fall over fence'
              (hold lf 4-CL) ——————————→

         (gaze at lf shoulder   )
Lee₅: **INDEX**-*lf shoulder* **#HURT**-*lf shoulder* **INDEX**-*lf shoulder*, **"WOW"+**

D. Key Illustrations

Pat

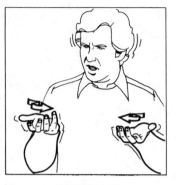

(2h)"WHAT"

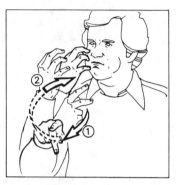

PURPLE⌣5:-CL'bruise on cheek'

WOW

Lee

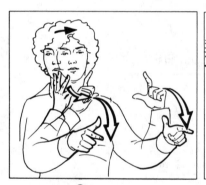

WATER⌣(2h)L:-CL@lf'lake'

B-CL-rt'hill next to lake'
L:-CL-lf'lake'

B-CL-cntr'front face of hill'
B-CL-cntr'hilltop'

V-CL@cntr'stand on hill'
B-CL-cntr'hilltop'

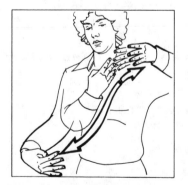

(2h)4-CL-lf
'fence on side of hill'

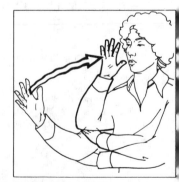

TREE-rt,upward-arc
'trees on side of hill'

1-CL-*cntr*
'ski down hill, weaving side to side'

V-CL-*lf* 'fall over fence'
4-CL-lf 'fence'

HURT-*lf shoulder*

E. Supplementary Illustrations

THAT-ONE-*rt*

THEREABOUTS

V:-CL-*rt*
1-CL'swerve to left to miss rabbit'

F. General Discussion: Locatives

The two previous discussions of locatives in Units 6 and 15 dealt with the way Signers can use classifiers, directional verbs, or verbs made at specific locations on the body to indicate the spatial relationship between two or more people, things, or places. Unit 15 also pointed out that, unlike English, ASL does not generally use separate signs (like the English prepositions 'at', 'in', 'under') to express locative relationships. Instead, ASL Signers efficiently use the signing space to indicate where things are and the locative relationship between those things.

For review, recall how classifiers were positioned and/or moved in the signing space to indicate the spatial relationship between various things in the following units:

Unit 5

3→CL-*rt*'car'   3→CL-*rt*'car stopped'
RED BURST-OF-*light*   3→CL'*car from left smash into left rear*'

Unit 6

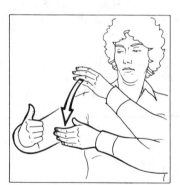 

A-CL-*rt*'trophy'   C-CL-*rt* } 'cup on table is
C-CL@*rt*'cup behind trophy*'   B↑-CL-*rt* } turned on its side'

Unit 14   **Unit 15**

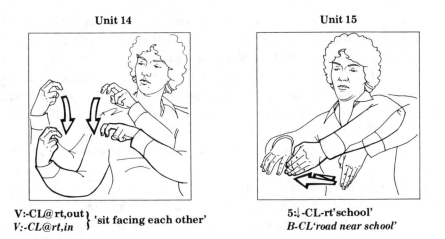

V:-CL@rt,out ⎫ 'sit facing each other'
V:-CL@rt,in ⎭

5:↓-CL-rt'school'
B-CL'road near school'

In each of the examples above, notice how the Signer uses both hands (two classifiers) to show a specific spatial relationship between the two things. The Signer can also convey locative information by using classifiers in a particular area of the signing space. For example, recall how classifiers in the following units indicated the spatial relationship between the things they were representing and something else:

Unit 7   **Unit 16**

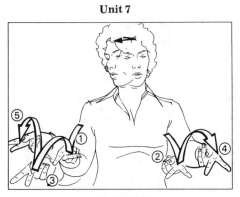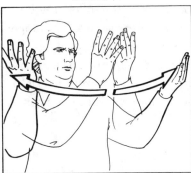

(2h)alt.V-CL
'kids lying on the floor'

(2h)4-CL-*up,lf* 'interpreters
in a line facing Signer'

Unit 14

(2h)alt.C-CL'pictures on wall'

(2h)A-CL*"sweep in rows"*-'trophies'

In the examples above, notice how the Signer uses a classifier in a particular area of the signing space to convey locative information of a more general nature. For example, using the **V-CL** in a lower part of the signing space (and gazing downward) shows that the 'kids are lying on the floor' (perhaps, on rugs or mats on the floor), not on a wall or ceiling or in mid-air. The 'interpreters' are located above the Signer, not on the floor; so they must be on some kind of platform or stage. The 'pictures' are located on the wall that the Signer set up earlier and are at eye-line or above, as is normal for pictures. The 'trophies' are in rows on top of each other, presumably on shelves of some kind.

Just as some classifiers can be moved as verbs in or to particular locations to show where something happens (e.g. **2-CL**'girls come up to me'), directional verbs can move from one spatial location to another to indicate where an action occurs. For example, recall how the verbs ____-**ASSEMBLE-TO**-____ and ____-**GO-TO**-____ indicated movement to 'Chicago' in Unit 10. A partial list of directional verbs like this can be found in Unit 22.

Similarly, verbs like **SHAVE-**____ and **HAVE-OPERATION-ON-**____ (see illustrations in Units 4 and 6) show where something happens by being made at a particular location on the Signer's body. Notice how the verb **#HURT-**____ is made at the Signer's left shoulder in the dialogue above. A partial list of verbs like this can be found in Unit 13.

Pointing with the index finger (indexing) is frequently used to show where something is or where something happens. The Signer may point to a 'real-life' location (like the Signer's cheek and left shoulder in the dialogue above) or to an established location in the signing space. For example, recall how Pat in Unit 15 described the location of a house in relation to the state school—or how Lee described the spatial relationship between the 'fancy home' and 'store' in Unit 23.

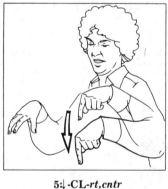

5:↓-CL-*rt,cntr*
INDEX-lf,cntr

Finally, as described in Unit 15, ASL tends *not* to use separate signs to express locative relationships in the way that English uses prepositions. However, ASL does have several, specifically locative signs (e.g. **IN, ON, UNDER, OPPOSITE-FROM, NEAR, BETWEEN, NEXT-TO-ON-THE-RIGHT**) which seem to be used when the Signer wants to focus on or emphasize a particular spatial relationship. In addition, sometimes a separate locative sign is used when there isn't any classifier or directional verb in the sentence which could be used to show the location of something.

Unfortunately, many sign vocabulary books have mislabeled signs like **GO-ACROSS** and **ENTER/GO-INTO** (often glossed as **ACROSS** or **OVER** and **INTO**, respectively) and have given the false impression that these signs are like English prepositions. However, observations of native Deaf Signers who use ASL show that these signs and others (e.g. those often labeled as **TO, BEHIND,** or **IN-FRONT-OF**) have other functions in the language. For example, some are verbs like **GO-ACROSS** and **ENTER/GO-INTO.** In addition, some of the supposedly 'preposition-like' signs in these vocabulary books (e.g. those labeled as **AT, AMONG,** or **AROUND**) are rarely, if ever, used by native Signers.

In summary, it is important to remember that whenever possible—which is most of the time!—ASL Signers generally use the signing space (via classifiers, directional verbs, indexing, etc.) to show the locative relationship between people, things, or places and to show the location of various actions or events.

G. Text Analysis

(puff.cheeks)wh-q

Pat$_1$:   (2h)"WHAT" HAPPEN INDEX-*Lee's rt cheek*   PURPLE 5:-CL'bruise on cheek' YOU

- **INDEX**-*Lee's rt.cheek*

    Notice that Pat points to a specific location on Lee's body (the right cheek) to indicate where something is. However, Pat then uses his/her own cheek as the location for the next sign.

- **PURPLE 5:-CL**'bruise on cheek'

    This is another example of two signs produced in such a way that they look like a single sign. Notice that the classifier **(5:-CL)** can occur in a number of different locations (eye, chin, shoulder, arm, etc.) to show where the 'bruise' occurs. Some Signers use the sign **BLUE 5:-CL** to express the same meaning.

(gaze down,lf   ) (gaze at 'hill'   )   q

Lee$_2$:   YOU KNOW   WATER (2h)L:-CL@*lf* 'lake' B-CL-*rt*'hillside next to lake', KNOW YOU
         (hold lf hand L:-CL) ———————————————————————→

- **WATER** (2h)**L:-CL@***lf* 'lake'   **B-CL-***rt*'hillside next to lake'
    (hold lf hand L;CL) ———————————————————————→

    Notice that the sign **WATER** and the (2h)**L:-CL** are produced in such a way that they look like a single sign. Notice that Pat establishes the 'lake' to the left and then uses it as a point of reference while indicating the relative location of the 'hill'.

	nodding	(gaze rt)	(gaze rt)		q
Pat₃:		THAT-ONE-*rt* FARM	THEREABOUTS-*rt*		THAT-ONE-*rt* ⌣YOU

B-CL-*lf* 'hillside' ⎯⎯⎯⎯⎯⎯⎯⎯⎯⎯⎯⎯⎯⎯⎯⎯→

⎯⎯⎯⎯⎯⎯⎯⎯⎯⎯⎯⎯⎯⎯⎯⎯⎯⎯⎯⎯⎯⎯⎯⎯⎯ q

- **THEREABOUTS**-*rt* ⎯⎯⎯⎯⎯⎯⎯⎯→ **THAT-ONE**-*rt* ⌣**YOU**

  B-CL-lf 'hillside' ⎯⎯⎯⎯⎯⎯⎯⎯⎯⎯⎯⎯⎯⎯⎯→

  The sign **THEREABOUTS** is used here to indicate an approximate location of the 'farm'. It is also used to indicate approximate dates, times, weights, prices, etc. Notice that Pat holds this sign to the right while locating the 'hillside' to the left, thus showing the location of the 'hillside' in relation to the 'farm'. Notice that the 'hillside' is located to Pat's left (***B-CL-lf***) — the same location used by Lee to establish the 'hillside' (**B-CL**-*rt*).

  Notice that Pat first responds affirmatively to Lee's question (*'nodding'*) but then asks a *'yes-no'* question to check and make sure they are discussing the same place.

	nodding	(gaze down,cntr)			br
Lee₃:	RIGHT +,	B-CL-*cntr*'front face of hill',	ME	V-CL@*cntr*'stand on hilltop'	

B-CL-cntr 'hilltop' ⎯⎯⎯⎯⎯⎯⎯⎯⎯⎯⎯⎯⎯⎯⎯⎯→

(gaze lf at 'fence')	(gaze rt)	br
(2h)4-CL-*lf*'fence on side of hill',	TREE-*rt,upward-arc*'trees on side of hill',	

(gaze down,cntr; look of'concentration'; body moving from side to side)
ME   SKI   1-CL-*cntr*'ski down hillside,weaving side to side'

(gaze down,cntr)		br

- **B-CL**-*cntr*'front of hill',   **ME**   **V-CL@***cntr*'stand on hilltop'

  B-CL-cntr 'hilltop' ⎯⎯⎯⎯⎯⎯⎯⎯⎯⎯⎯⎯⎯⎯⎯⎯→

  Notice that the Signer has shifted perspective from describing the hillside at a distance (Lee₂) to placing him/herself in the scene. See Units 21 and 23 for a discussion of how Signers shift perspective.

  Notice also that the Signer positions the **V-CL** *on top of* the **B-CL** (left hand) to show the spatial relationship between the skier (Lee) and the hill.

  (gaze lf at 'fence'   ) (gaze rt)

- (2h)4-**CL**-*lf*'fence on side of hill',   **TREE**-*rt,upward-arc*'trees on side of **l**

  Notice how Lee shows that the 'fence' is on the left side of the hill and the 'trees' are on the right.

  Notice also that Lee describes this scene as s/he saw it from the top of the hill, thus maintaining the change of perspective mentioned above.

- **1-CL**-*cntr*'ski down hillside,weaving side to side'

    > Notice how the location of this classifier shows that Lee skiied 'down the hill'. Also notice how the movement of the classifier details the manner or type of movement—'weaving side to side'.

Lee$_4$:   "PSHAW", 1-CL-*cntr*'ski down hillside', $\overline{\text{RABBIT,}}^{\text{t}}$

(look of 'fright'   )
V:-CL-*rt*'hop from trees in front of me'   **ME** 1-CL'swerve to lf to miss rabbit'

(gaze lf, 'shocked'   )
(2h)**4-CL**-*lf*'fence' **V-CL**-*lf*'fall over fence'
(hold *lf 4-CL*) ————————————→

- **V:-CL**-*rt*'hop from trees in front of me'

    > As mentioned in Unit 5, this classifier can represent a cat, dog, mouse, etc. In this instance, it represents the 'rabbit'. Notice how the classifier provides locative information— the **V:-CL** moves from the Signer's right (the 'trees') across the face of the hill in front of the Signer.

- **1-CL**'swerve to lf to miss rabbit'

    > Notice how this classifier provides locative information— the Signer swerves to the left (i.e. toward the fence and away from the rabbit).

(gaze lf, 'shocked'   )
- (2h)**4-CL**-*lf*'fence'   **V-CL**-*lf*'fall over fence'
    (hold *lf 4-CL*) ————————————————→

    > Notice that Lee re-establishes the fence to the left and then holds the left *4-CL* in order to describe the locative relationship between it and the skiier (represented by the **V-CL**). The **V-CL** then 'falls over' the *4-CL* to show that the 'skiier fell over the fence'.

Lee$_5$:   (gaze at lf shoulder   )
    INDEX-*lf shoulder*   **#HURT**-*lf shoulder* **INDEX**-*lf shoulder*,   "WOW" +

(gaze at lf shoulder)
- **INDEX**-*lf shoulder* **# HURT**-*lf shoulder*

    > Notice how both of these signs are made on or near a specific part of the body, thus providing specific locative information about where the injury is. Notice also that the loan sign **# HURT** is one of the verbs which can indicate that the action occurs at a particular location on the body.

H. Sample Drills

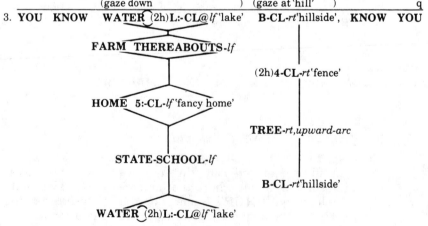

```
                                      (puff.cheeks                           )wh-q
1. (2h)"WHAT"  HAPPEN    PURPLE 5:-CL'bruise on rt cheek'   YOU

                         BLUE 5:-CL'bruise on lf shoulder'

                              5:-CL'bruise on lf forearm'

                    PURPLE 5:-CL'bruise on lf cheek'

                              5:-CL'bruise on rt thigh'

                    BLUE 5:-CL'bruise on rt cheek'

                         5:-CL'bruise on forehead'

                    PURPLE 5:-CL'bruise on rt cheek'
```

```
         t                          (look of 'fright'    ) (gaze lf, 'shocked'                        )
2. RABBIT,  V:-CL-rt'hop from rt'   ME  1-CL'swerve to lf' (2h)4-CL-lf'fence'   V-CL-lf'fall over  fence'
                                                           (hold lf 4-CL) ————————————————————————————►

                                                                       1-CL-lf'ski next to fence'

         MOUSE

                                                                       1-CL-lf'crash into fence'

         CAT

                                                                       V-CL-lf'fall in front of fence'

         #DOG

                                                                       V-CL-lf'land on top of fence'

         RABBIT

                                                                       V-CL-lf'fall over fence'
```

```
              (gaze down                ) (gaze at 'hill'    )                    q
3. YOU  KNOW    WATER (2h)L:-CL@lf'lake'   B-CL-rt'hillside',  KNOW  YOU

         FARM  THEREABOUTS-lf

                                          (2h)4-CL-rt'fence'

         HOME  5:-CL-lf'fancy home'

                                          TREE-rt,upward-arc

         STATE-SCHOOL-lf

                                          B-CL-rt'hillside'

         WATER (2h)L:-CL@lf'lake'
```

I. Video Notes

If you have access to the videotape package designed to accompany these texts, you will notice the following:

- In Pat's first turn, she uses a modulated form of the sign **PURPLE**—which indicates that the bruise is 'dark' purple.

- During Lee's third turn, he carefully checks with Pat (by looking at her) after setting up each referent to make sure she clearly recognizes where each thing is in relation to the other things—the hill, where Lee was standing, the fence, and the line of trees. Then, when the 'stage is set', Lee describes what happened.

- In Lee$_4$, he uses a two-handed variant of the sign **RABBIT** (made in neutral space) rather than the one-handed (or two-handed) form made at the side(s) of the head.

- Notice the difference between the way Pat signs #**HURT** in her last turn and the way Lee signs #**HURT** in his last turn. Lee's is stressed, meaning 'very hurt'.

Unit 25

Pluralization

A. Synopsis

Pat and Lee are dining out. Pat asks if Lee is going to college next year. Lee says that s/he hasn't decided but that if s/he goes to college, it'll be NTID. There are a lot of different things Lee can major in; plus they have hills there for hiking, skiing, etc. Lee's only objection is that it's cold in Rochester. Pat agrees and says that one time s/he went there with no coat and everybody stared. So s/he hunted around for a clothing store and ended up buying a coat that fit perfectly. Lee says that Pat was lucky.

B. Cultural Information: The National Technical Institute for the Deaf (NTID)

In 1965, a law was passed which created a National Technical Institute for the Deaf (NTID). The site chosen for this special institute was Rochester, New York, on the campus of the Rochester Institute of Technology (RIT). After several years of planning, the first group of 71 students enrolled in 1968. Now there are approximately 900 students enrolled at NTID. The primary purpose of the institute is to provide educational training opportunities for deaf students in technological areas.

The historical underemployment or unemployment of deaf people was a primary reason for the creation of NTID. In response to this need, NTID not only provides academic training for its students but also provides academic career counseling and job placement counseling. In fact, as of 1979, 95% of NTID graduates who had sought jobs had found employment; 94% had been hired at a level appropriate for their training, and 84% had been hired in business and industry.

Because NTID is located on the campus of RIT (and, in fact, is one of the nine colleges of RIT), the deaf students there frequently have the option of being "integrated" with the hearing students at RIT. To deal with this situation, NTID provides a number of support services for its students. Some of these services are: providing interpreters for NTID students, and providing note-takers in classes.

For further information, contact: NTID, RIT, Public Information Office, One Lomb Memorial Drive, Rochester, New York 14623.

C. Dialogue

Pat

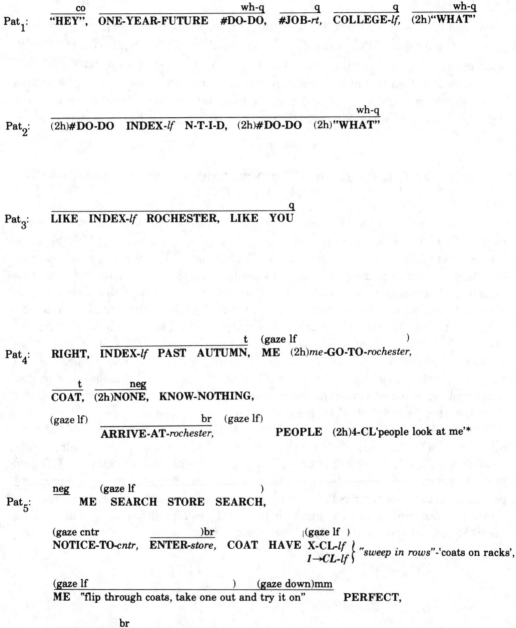

	co		wh-q		q		q		wh-q

Pat₁: "HEY", ONE-YEAR-FUTURE #DO-DO, #JOB-*rt*, COLLEGE-*lf*, (2h)"WHAT"

<u>   wh-q</u>

Pat₂: (2h)#DO-DO INDEX-*lf* N-T-I-D, (2h)#DO-DO (2h)"WHAT"

                                 q

Pat₃: LIKE INDEX-*lf* ROCHESTER, LIKE YOU

                                t   (gaze lf   )

Pat₄: RIGHT, INDEX-*lf* PAST AUTUMN, ME (2h)*me*-GO-TO-*rochester*,

       t   neg

COAT, (2h)NONE, KNOW-NOTHING,

(gaze lf)   br   (gaze lf)

         ARRIVE-AT-*rochester*,   PEOPLE (2h)4-CL'people look at me'*

      neg   (gaze lf   )

Pat₅: ME SEARCH STORE SEARCH,

(gaze cntr   )br |(gaze lf)

NOTICE-TO-*cntr*, ENTER-*store*, COAT HAVE X-CL-*lf* } *"sweep in rows"*-'coats on racks',

                                           1→CL-*lf* }

(gaze lf   )   (gaze down)mm

ME "flip through coats, take one out and try it on" PERFECT,

             br

BUY FINISH, RELIEVED

Pat₆: (Facial signal that means 'Yeah, I know that')

Lee

Lee₁: (2h)"WELL", NOT-YET DECIDE ME <u>INDEX-*rt*</u> —————→ INDEX-*rt* —————→)
        (gaze rt&lf↔
        INDEX-*lf* —————→ INDEX-*lf*

        <u>   (gaze rt)cond</u>
        SUPPOSE COLLEGE-*rt*,   (2h)*me*-GO-TO-*rt*   N-T-I-D   ME

        <u>   nod</u>
Lee₂: (2h)"WELL" SPECIALTY-FIELD DIFFERENT++-*arc*,   INDEX-*lf thumb*   PHOTOGRAPHY,

        (gaze at lf index) <u>nod</u>   (gaze at lf middle finger) <u>nod</u>
        INDEX-*lf index*   ART,   INDEX-*lf middle finger*   MATH,   LIST-OF-ITEMS   (2h)"WELL"

                            (gaze rt)   <u>(gaze rt   )</u>   <u>mm</u>
Lee₃: (2h)"WELL" "SO-SO", INDEX-*rt* HAVE ROCK B-CL-*rt*'hill' —————→ SEVERAL,
                                                   B-CL-'hill'

        <u>   mm+nodding</u>   <u>rhet.q</u>
        CAN SKI, WALK VARIOUS-THINGS "WELL",   PROBLEM ONE,

        INDEX-*rt* COLD "WOW" COLD* INDEX-*rt*,   (2h)"PSHAW"

                                                          <u>t</u>   <u>wh-q</u>   <u>q</u>   <u>wh-q</u>
Lee₄: "OH-MY", PEOPLE (2h)4-CL'people look at you',   #DO-DO,   DON'T-CARE,   (2h"WHAT"

Lee₅: LUCKY‿YOU

D. Key Illustrations

Pat

(2h)# DO-DO

KNOW-NOTHING

(2h)alt.4-CL'people look at me'

X-CL-*lf* ⎫
1→CL-*lf* ⎬ *"sweep in rows"*

PERFECT

RELIEVED

Lee

"SO-SO"

DIFFERENT+ + + -*arc*

LIST-OF-ITEMS

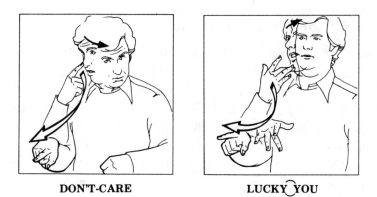

DON'T-CARE

LUCKY‿YOU

E. Supplementary Illustrations

NOT-YET

SUPPOSE

SPECIALTY-FIELD

SEVERAL

VARIOUS-THINGS

NOTICE-TO-*rt*

F. General Discussion: Pluralization

The two previous discussions of pluralization (Units 7 and 16) explored a variety of ways that ASL Signers show there is more than one of something—i.e. that the referent is plural. Many of these ways involve some form of repetition. For example, singular classifiers and pronouns, some nouns and adjectives, and many verbs will indicate plurality by being repeated in different locations. However, some signs are inherently plural—like the noun **PEOPLE**, the plural classifier **2-CL**, and the plural pronoun **US-THREE**—and do not need repetition. This discussion will review these and other ways to show that something is plural as well as consider the similarities between several of the plural modulations.

One obvious way to show that something is plural is to use a specific number sign like **TWO** or **FIVE** or a non-specific number sign like **FEW, SEVERAL,** or **MANY.** Often (especially among young Signers), this sign will occur *before* the noun. When the number sign occurs *after* the noun (as in **BOOK TWO***), it is usually stressed and shows that the number has special significance—as it would have if you had to read *two* books in one night for a homework assignment.

Handshapes which represent specific numbers also occur as a part of several other types of signs—for example, time adverbs like **TWO-WEEK-PAST** and **THREE-YEAR-FUTURE,** pronouns like **US-THREE** and **YOU-FOUR,** nouns like **TWO-HOUR** and **FOUR-DAY,** and classifiers like **2-CL** and **4-CL.**

| TWO-WEEK-PAST | US-THREE | 2-CL'come up to me from rt' |

As described in Unit 14, the '4' and '5' handshapes also occur in various classifiers that do not indicate specifically '4' or '5' referents. For example, when both hands (with either the '4' or '5' handshape, fingers upright) are used *together,* they no longer represent a specific number of individuals, but represent a group of *many* individuals—as seen in the 'row of interpreters' in Unit 16.

Plural classifiers like **5↓-CL, 5↓wg-CL,** and **5:↓-CL** also indicate that the referent is a group of many people, animals, or things. For example, signing **WOMAN 5:↓-CL** would indicate that the referent of the sign **WOMAN** is a large group of women. Similarly, signing **BIRD (2h)4:-CL'in** an arc facing Signer' would indicate that the referent of the sign **BIRD** is a large group of birds. In general, when both hands are used with these classifiers, it indicates that the group is *very* large.

Another way to indicate that a referent is plural is to repeat the noun itself (usually once). However, this is only possible with a small number of nouns—like **SENTENCE, LANGUAGE, RULE, MEANING, SPECIALTY-FIELD, AREA, ROOM/BOX, HOUSE, STREET/WAY,** and **STATUE.** And even these nouns are not always repeated when they refer to a plural referent. For example, when a number sign modifies the noun (e.g. **TWO HOUSE**), the noun usually is not repeated—unless the Signer wants to assign spatial locations to those things for later reference. (Also notice that **SPECIALTY-FIELD** is not repeated in the dialogue above although its referent is plural. Instead, the adjective which follows it— **DIFFERENT**—is repeated in an arc to indicate plurality.)

Singular classifiers are always modulated to show plurality if the referent is plural. For example, it would be *ungrammatical* to sign ***THREE PENCIL 1→CL@***rt*. Singular classifiers are pluralized by repeating them in different locations. (We consider the *"sweep"* movement to be an assimilated form of repetition. It involves movement across the signing space and thus, in a sense, encompasses many locations.) The basic plural modulations of singular classifiers are illustrated below. Recall that the *"sweep"* modulations generally indicate a larger number of referents than the modulations which involve separate repetitions.

(2h)alt.A-CL

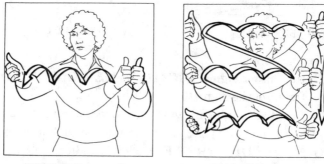

(2h)A-CL*"in a row"*   (2h)A-CL*"in rows"*

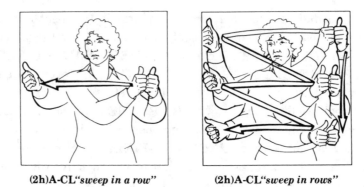

(2h)A-CL*"sweep in a row"*   (2h)A-CL*"sweep in rows"*

Singular pronouns will also be made plural if the referent is plural. This is done either with separate repetitions of the pronoun (e.g. **INDEX+ + -rt**) or with the 'arc' movement (e.g. **POSS-***arc-rt;* **YOURSELVES**). Thus, for example, signing **BOY INDEX-***arc-rt* will indicate that the referent of the sign **BOY** is plural.

As described in Unit 16, verbs can also show that something is plural. For example, the modulations written as *"each"*, *"all"*, *"specified"*, and *"unspecified"* (see Units 18 or 27) indicate that either the subject or object is plural. In each case, the verb moves toward or from different locations in space. (Like the 'sweep' movement of classifiers and 'arc' movement of pronouns, the smooth arc movement seen in the *"all"* modulation of verbs is considered to be a movement across several/many locations.)

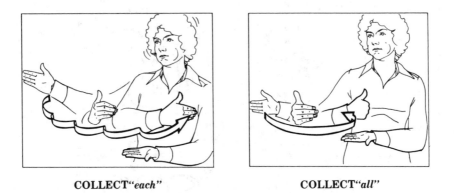

COLLECT*"each"*   COLLECT*"all"*

So, for example, if the Signer signed **PICTURE, ME COLLECT***"each"*, it would
be clear that the referent of the sign **PICTURE** is plural.

Finally, some verbs always indicate that the subject is plural (actually 'many'). Usually these verbs are made with the '4' or '5' handshapes. For example, the signs **ASSEMBLE-TO-____** and **DISPERSE-FROM-____** indicate the subject is plural and cannot be used if it is singular. Thus, signing **GIRL ASSEMBLE-TO-***cntr* would clearly indicate that the referent of the sign **GIRL** is plural. (Also notice how the *'puff.cheeks'* signal in the illustration below 'agrees with' the plurality of the referent.)

ASSEMBLE-TO-*cntr*

In summary, many different kinds of signs can show that something is plural—including classifiers, pronouns, nouns, adjectives, verbs, and number signs. Whereas some signs are themselves plural (e.g. **US-TWO, 3-CL**), other signs require some type of plural modulation to show that the referent is plural. In general, all of these modulations involve some kind of repetition. This includes the 'sweeping' or 'arc-like' modulations that occur with classifiers, pronouns, and verbs.

G. Text Analysis

<pre>
                     <u>co</u>   <u>wh-q</u>   <u>q</u>   <u>q</u>   <u>wh-q</u>
Pat₁: "HEY", ONE-YEAR-FUTURE #DO-DO, #JOB-rt, COLLEGE-lf, (2h)"WHAT"

               <u>q</u>   <u>q</u>
     • #JOB-rt,   COLLEGE-lf
</pre>

> Notice that these two signs are assigned different spatial locations. This right and left alternation often occurs when asking about options or preferences.

<pre>
                                        (gaze rt&lf↔   )
Lee₁: (2h)"WELL", NOT-YET DECIDE ME INDEX-rt ──────→ INDEX-rt ──────→
                                              INDEX-lf──────→INDEX-lf
</pre>

<pre>
            (gaze rt   )cond
     SUPPOSE COLLEGE-rt, (2h)me-GO-TO-rt N-T-I-D ME

        (gaze rt & lf   )
     • INDEX-rt ──────→ INDEX-rt ──────→
            INDEX-lf──────→ INDEX-lf
</pre>

> Notice that Lee uses the same spatial locations assigned by Pat with the signs **#JOB**-*rt* (*INDEX-lf*) and **COLLEGE**-*lf* (**INDEX**-*rt*). Notice also that Lee gazes back and forth between the two locations while indexing them.

              <u>(gaze rt   )cond</u>
- **SUPPOSE COLLEGE-***rt*

    This is the *condition* portion of a conditional statement. Units 10 and 19 describe the non-manual behaviors used to signal a conditional. Notice that the sign **COLLEGE** is produced to Lee's right—the same spatial location it was assigned by Pat.

                                                                    <u>nod</u>

Lee$_2$: (2h)"WELL" SPECIALTY-FIELD DIFFERENT++*-arc,* INDEX-*lf thumb* PHOTOGRAPHY,

(gaze at lf index)   <u>nod</u>   (gaze at lf middle finger)   <u>nod</u>
INDEX-*lf index*   ART, INDEX-*lf middle finger*   MATH, LIST-OF-ITEMS (2h)"WELL"

- **SPECIALTY-FIELD**

    In high schools and colleges, this sign is generally used to refer to a student's major in college. Notice that this noun is not repeated here even though its referent is plural. Instead, the next sign indicates this fact.

- **DIFFERENT+ + -***arc*

    Notice that the repetition of this sign in an arc indicates that there are a number of different 'majors'.

                            <u>nod</u>   <u>nod</u>
- **INDEX-***lf thumb* **PHOTOGRAPHY,** **INDEX-***lf index* **ART,**

    'Counting' the fingers of the passive hand is a common way of listing things in ASL. (See the *General Discussion* section in Unit 21.) It also assigns each referent to a specific location (i.e. to a specific finger). Thus, if later in the conversation Lee wanted to discuss **ART**, s/he would point to (index) the left index finger.

    Also notice the head nod that occurs with each referent and the pause between each item in the list.

- **LIST-OF-ITEMS**

    Notice that this sign also indicates that the referent of the sign **SPECIALTY-FIELD** is plural.

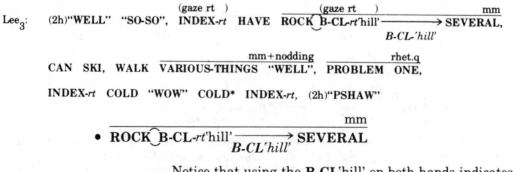

                  (gaze rt)   (gaze rt   )   mm
Lee$_3$: (2h)"WELL" "SO-SO", INDEX-*rt* HAVE ROCK B-CL-*rt*'hill'⟶ SEVERAL,
                                                        B-CL-'hill'

                            <u>mm+nodding</u>   <u>rhet.q</u>
CAN SKI, WALK VARIOUS-THINGS "WELL", PROBLEM ONE,

INDEX-*rt* COLD "WOW" COLD* INDEX-*rt,* (2h)"PSHAW"

                                       <u>mm</u>
- **ROCK B-***rt*'hill'⟶ **SEVERAL**
                      B-CL'hill'

    Notice that using the **B-CL**'hill' on both hands indicates that there is more than one 'hill'. The Signer also shows this with the sign **SEVERAL.**

Notice the non-manual *'mm'* signal which conveys the meanings 'regular', 'normal', or 'usual'. This indicates that the hills are not large, but are just 'regular, old hills'.

$$\overline{\text{SKI, \ WALK, \ VARIOUS-THINGS \ "WELL"}}^{\text{mm+ nodding}}$$

- **SKI, WALK, VARIOUS-THINGS "WELL"**

  The sign **VARIOUS-THINGS** often occurs after items on a list. Here it indicates that there are a number of things that one can do in the hills besides 'skiing' and 'walking'. Again, notice the pauses between the items on the list (**SKI, WALK,**) and notice the *'mm'* signal—which indicates that the 'various things' one can do are not out of the ordinary.

$$\overline{\text{PROBLEM \ ONE,}}^{\text{rhet.q}}$$

- **PROBLEM ONE,**

  This is a rhetorical question. Notice that Lee does not use a sign like **WHY, WHAT,** or **REASON** to signal the rhetorical question. Rather the non-manual *'rhet.q'* signal is the only indication of the rhetorical question. The specific non-manual behaviors in this signal are described in Units 10 and 19.

Pat$_4$: $\overline{\text{RIGHT, \ INDEX-}lf \ \text{PAST \ AUTUMN,}}^{\text{t}}$ ME $\overline{\text{(2h)}me\text{-GO-TO-}rochester,}^{\text{(gaze lf}}$)

$\overline{\text{COAT,}}^{\text{t}}$ $\overline{\text{(2h)NONE,}}^{\text{neg}}$ KNOW-NOTHING,

(gaze lf) $\overline{\text{ARRIVE-AT-}rochester,}^{\text{br \ (gaze lf)}}$ PEOPLE   (2h)4-CL'people look at me'*

- **(2h)***me***-GO-TO-***rochester*

  Notice that this sign moves toward the location previously assigned to Rochester (Pat's left) by Lee (Lee$_1$).

- **PEOPLE** (2h)4-CL'people look at me'*

  Both of these signs are plural. The sign **PEOPLE** is a plural noun, and the sign (2h)4-CL'people look at me' is a plural classifier used as a verb. Notice that the verb is made with both hands, suggesting that *'many* people looked at' Pat. Also notice that the sign is stressed.

  In this case, the **4-CL** functions like a directional verb. It is clear that 'people' is the subject and Pat ('me') is the object. Notice that Lee also uses the **4-CL** as a directional verb (Lee$_4$).

Pat₅:
    <u>neg</u>   (gaze lf   )
    ME   SEARCH STORE SEARCH,

(gaze cntr   )br |(gaze lf)
NOTICE-TO-*cntr*, ENTER-*store*, COAT HAVE X-CL-*lf* ⎱
                                      1→CL-*lf* ⎰ *"sweep in rows"*-'coats on racks',

(gaze lf   )   (gaze down)mm
ME   "flip through coats, take one out and try it on"   PERFECT,

             br
BUY   FINISH, RELIEVED

- X-CL-*lf* ⎱ *"sweep in rows"*-'coats on racks'
- 1→CL-*lf* ⎰

  > Notice in the illustration how these two classifiers are positioned together to provide the locative information that the coats are on hangers (**X-CL**) which are on racks (**1→CL**). Notice also how the *"sweep in rows"* modulation indicates that there were *many* coats on each rack and that there were several racks.

  (gaze lf   )   (gaze down)mm
- **ME** "flip through coats, take one out and try it on"   **PERFECT**

  > Notice the *'mm'* signal that accompanies the Signer's mimed routine of looking through the coats on the rack and trying one on.

- **PERFECT**

  > This sign (made with 'F' handshapes) is often used to show that something 'fits perfectly'.

Pat₆: (Facial signal that means 'Yeah, I know that')

               This facial signal (sometimes written as **UH-HUH** or **YEAH-I-KNOW-THAT**) involves a rapid, repeated wrinkling of the nose—often on only one side of the nose. Addressees frequently use this signal to give feedback to the Signer. (See the Video Notes in Unit 19 for another instance where this signal occurred.)

mead

Sample Drills

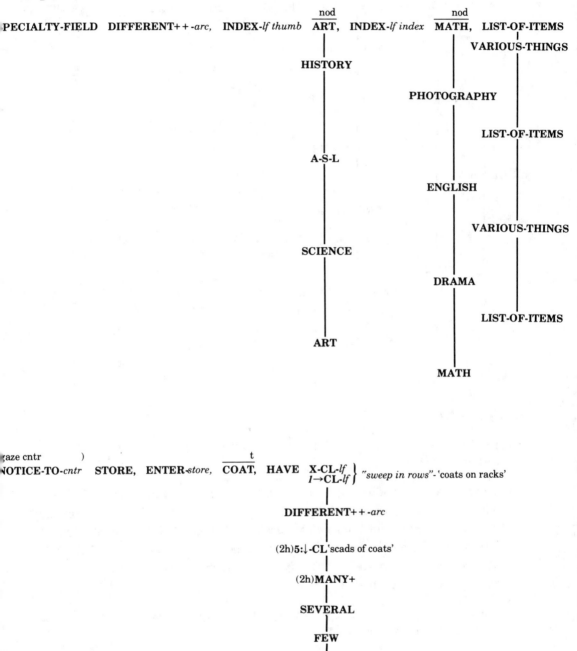

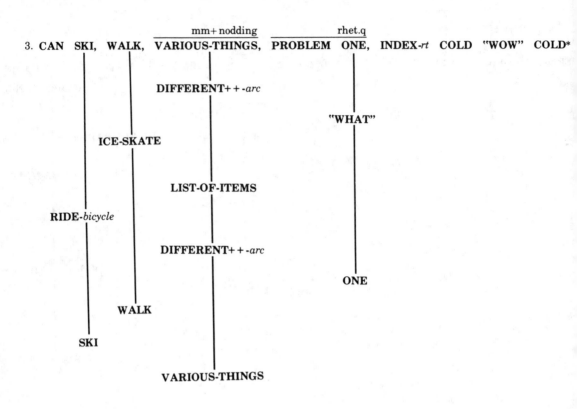

3. CAN SKI, WALK, VARIOUS-THINGS, PROBLEM ONE, INDEX-*rt* COLD "WOW" COLD*

I. Video Notes

If you have access to the videotape package designed to accompany these tapes, you will notice the following:

- The two examples of listing behavior in Lee's second and third turn. Notice the pauses after each item in both lists and the signs which are often used to 'extend' a list (like saying 'and so on' or 'etcetera') — **LIST-OF-ITEMS** and **VARIOUS-THINGS**. Also notice the 'reduced' form of the signs **PHOTOGRAPHY, ART,** and **MATH** in the first list. This gives them each 'one beat' and maintains the rhythmic quality of the list.

- The sign **SKI** in Lee$_3$ (made with two 'X' handshapes) is different than the sign **SKI** that Lee uses in Unit 24.

- In Lee$_4$, the Signer uses a two-handed form of the sign **DON'T-CARE.**

- In Pat's fifth turn, she moves both classifier handshapes outward rather than only the dominant hand as pictured in the illustration. Also notice that she uses the sign **EXACT** rather than the sign **PERFECT.** In this context, they have the same meaning.

Unit 26

Temporal Aspect

A. Synopsis

Pat and Lee are in a restaurant and Pat tells Lee that their friend, ⚠ , is seriously ill. It seems that last week he was really working hard—day and night—and a few days ago he got really sick. ⚠ had to go to the hospital and be examined, but the doctor hasn't told him what's wrong yet. Pat says that their friend's wife has been crying and crying for three days and Pat is afraid she'll have a breakdown. Lee suggests that they go visit ⚠ .

B. Cultural Information: Deaf Patients in Hospitals

In the past, Deaf individuals have had and often still have a somewhat difficult time obtaining adequate and appropriate medical services in hospitals. While this situation is changing in many hospitals, it continues to be an unnecessary cause of anxiety and fear for many Deaf people. Some of the difficulties encountered are due to a lack of sensitivity and awareness on the part of the hospital staff. Consider, for example, the following situations:

— a Deaf person who is right-handed is given an intravenous infusion in the right arm and, thus, can neither sign nor write.
— a Deaf person is prepared for surgery and, after sedation is administered, the doctor explains the upcoming procedure. The sedative, however, affects the patient's eyesight and s/he does not understand what is happening.
— a Deaf person rings for the nurse, but the nurse answers via an intercom system which the Deaf person cannot hear.

These examples illustrate some of the difficulties encountered by Deaf patients in hospitals. There are some obvious solutions to these problems such as training members of the hospital staff to use Sign Language or employing qualified interpreters. One of the best ways of dealing with such problems would be to hire qualified Deaf personnel. And, in fact, an increasing number of programs are making available to Deaf individuals the training and background needed to become nurses, nurse's aides, and medical technicians or to work in other health-related areas.

C. Dialogue

Pat

<pre>
                    co   t   q
Pat₁: "UMMM"+ KNOW-THAT YOU △ , BECOME-SICK, KNOW-THAT YOU
</pre>

<pre>
              neg   nodding
Pat₂: "NO-NO" WORSE, SICK BECOME-SERIOUSLY-ILL
</pre>

<pre>
                                                        q   nod
Pat₃: YOU KNOW INDEX-rt WORK #VR INDEX-rt,

        ONE-WEEK-PAST SOMETHING IMPORTANT,

                              'intently'
        INDEX-rt △ INDEX-rt WORK"over time" ALL-WEEK,

                                                           sta
        ALL-DAY⌢ALL-NIGHT ALL-DAY⌢ALL-NIGHT WORK"over & over again",

                   t
        FEW-DAY-PAST, BECOME-SERIOUSLY-ILL THROW-rt HOSPITAL
</pre>

<pre>
                        (gaze lf, lean lf   ) 'intently'
Pat₄: (2h)"WELL", DOCTOR (2h)SEARCH-body(lf)"over time"

        (body shift rt, gaze lf 'anxiously')   neg
        △ WAIT-lf "long time",   NOT-YET doctor(lf)-INFORM-john(rt)
</pre>

<pre>
                          br   sta
Pat₅: "WELL" UP-TIL-NOW THREE-DAY, WIFE (2h)CRY"long time",

                               nodding
        ME FEEL BREAK-DOWN FEEL ME
</pre>

<pre>
        puff.cheeks+nodding
Pat₆: YES++
</pre>

Lee

Lee₁: **INDEX**-*lf* **TEND-TO** **BE-SICK**"*over time*"

               wh-q
Lee₂: $\overline{\text{HOWwg}}$

                            wh-q   q
Lee₃: **WOW,** $\overline{\textbf{WRONG+ "WHAT",}}$ $\overline{\textbf{INDEX-}lf\ \textbf{KNOW+}\ \textbf{INDEX-}lf}$

                    q
Lee₄: $\overline{\textbf{WIFE}\ \ \textbf{\#OK}}$

                        (gaze lf)   wh-q (br squint)q
Lee₅: $\overline{\textbf{WHY} \frown \textbf{NOT}\ \ \textbf{US-TWO}\ \ \textbf{FROM-}here\textbf{-GO-TO-}lf\ \ \textbf{HOSPITAL}\ \ \textbf{(2h)NOW,}}$ $\overline{\textbf{WANTwg}}$

D. Key Illustrations

Pat

(top row)

WORSE

BECOME-SERIOUSLY-ILL

'intently'
_____
WORK"over time"

ALL-WEEK

sta
_____
WORK"over & over again"

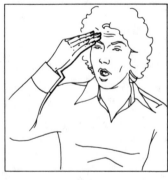

WAIT"long time"

(2h)CRY"long time"

KNOW

Lee

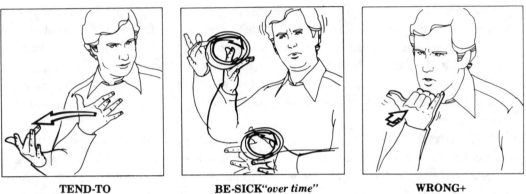

TEND-TO   **BE-SICK***"over time"*   **WRONG+**

E. Supplementary Illustrations

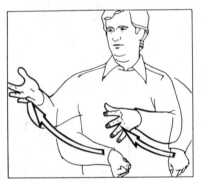

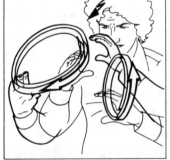

THROW-*rt*   **'intently'**   **BREAK-DOWN**

                        (2h)SEARCH-*body"over time"*

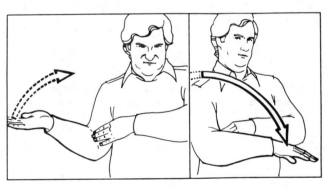

ALL-DAY   **ALL-NIGHT**

F. General Discussion: Temporal Aspect

The two previous discussions (Units 8 and 17) presented four verb modulations that convey information about the duration or frequency of an event. Since linguistic research in this area of ASL is in the beginning stages, it is likely that additional modulations for temporal aspect will be described in the future. Given that, the discussions of temporal aspect presented in these texts will need to be modified and expanded in the future when more information becomes available.

The four modulations presented in the two previous discussions are illustrated below. The approximate meanings are given in italics, followed by a description of the modulation.

Notice that the *"over time"* and *"regularly"* modulations both include the meaning 'regularly' in some contexts. Note, however, that the English word 'regularly' is ambiguous: it can refer to the 'steady repetition' of an event, or it can mean that the occurrence of the action is 'normal' or 'routine'. Both of these meanings seem to fit both modulations in some contexts.

(a) *"over time"* *(continually; regularly; for awhile)*

　　This inflection is made with a repeated, circular movement.

(b) *"regularly"* *(frequently; repeatedly; a lot; with active focus)*

　　This inflection is made with a repeated, small (non-tense) straight-line movement.[1]

---

[1]Another inflection that has a meaning like 'to do something so often that it seems like it never stops; incessantly' is similar to the inflection described in (b). However, the movement of this inflection is very tense, small, and rapid.

(c) *"long time" (for a prolonged period of time)*

This inflection is made with a slower, repeated, elliptical movement—composed of a rounded 'thrust' and 'return'.

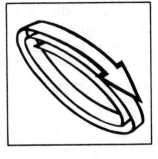

(d) *"over and over again" (prolonged, repeated focus)*

This inflection is made with (a) a repeated cycle—composed of a tense straight-line movement (short 'hold' at end of 'thrust', followed by an arc-like transitional movement back to the starting place) and (b) a forward rocking motion of the body and/or head with each 'thrust'.

Compare the following four illustrations to make sure you can clearly distinguish each modulation.

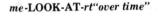

me-**LOOK-AT**-*rt"over time"*

me-**LOOK-AT**-*rt"regularly"*

me-**LOOK-AT**-*rt"long time"*

me-**LOOK-AT**-*rt"over & over again"*

Remember that the Signer's *perception of* (feelings about) the length or frequency of the event plays a major role in determining which modulation will be used. This is because the same event can be described in several different ways. For example, crying for an hour can be viewed as crying for a long time (*"long time"*) or it can be viewed as crying for awhile (*"over time"*).

CRY*"over time"*

CRY*"long time"*

Recall Unit 8 in which Lee states that s/he applied for a job and has been waiting 'a long time' to see whether the application was accepted. It could be that Lee applied just two weeks ago—but two weeks can seem like a long time if you are waiting for something important to happen!

Not all verbs can be modulated in each of the four ways described above. Some verbs which can be modulated in each of these ways are:

___-GO-TO-___	___-ASK-TO-___	___-FORCE-___
___-RUN-TO-___	___-HIT-___	___-BLAME-___
___-THROW-AT-___	___-GIVE-TO-___	___-BAWL-OUT-___
___-INSULT-___	___-INFORM-___	___-BOTHER-___
___-SEND-TO-___	___-LOOK-AT-___	TELL-LIE
___-PREACH-TO-___	___-TEACH-___	PLAY
___-PICK-ON-___	___-TEASE-___	WRITE
___-MAKE-FUN-OF-___	___-TTY-CALL-TO-___	ANALYZE
___-BLAME-___	___-TELL-TO-___	STUDY
		MEETING

You should also be aware that some non-manual signals only occur with certain modulations and not with others. For example, in the context of 'working', the *'pursed lips'* signal would add the meaning of working 'fast' or 'breezing through' the work. But this facial signal would not make sense if the verb (**WORK**) had the modulation "over & over again"—since, logically, you can't 'breeze through' something that is taxing and has to be focused on again and again.

Examine the following illustrations and notice the different non-manual signals. Consider how these signals 'make sense' with the modulations they accompany.

Under the gloss for each illustration, note the approximate meaning in English—which includes the meaning of the non-manual signal and the temporal modulation. (The 'sta' signal is described in the *Text Analysis*—Lee₃).

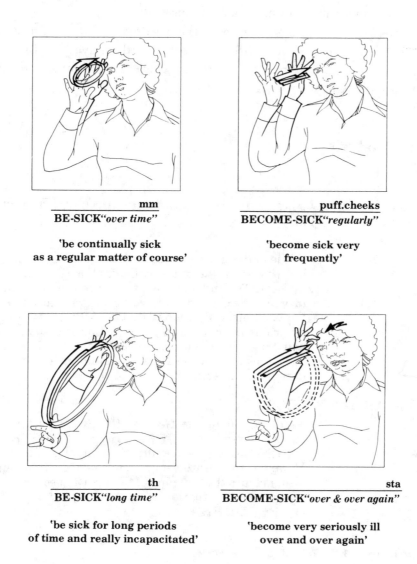

<table>
<tr><td style="text-align:center">mm
BE-SICK"*over time*"

'be continually sick
as a regular matter of course'</td><td style="text-align:center">puff.cheeks
BECOME-SICK"*regularly*"

'become sick very
frequently'</td></tr>
<tr><td style="text-align:center">th
BE-SICK"*long time*"

'be sick for long periods
of time and really incapacitated'</td><td style="text-align:center">sta
BECOME-SICK"*over & over again*"

'become very seriously ill
over and over again'</td></tr>
</table>

Notice that the sign glossed as **SICK** (which makes it look like an adjective) actually includes the meaning of the verb 'to be' or 'to become'. Thus, it can be modulated in the ways shown above. Adjectives like these are called *predicate adjectives*. Other examples are **(BE/BECOME)WRONG**, **(BE/BECOME)-FRUSTRATED**, and **(BE/BECOME/SILLY**.

In summary, the four modulations described above provide information about the duration or frequency of an event. The choice of which modulation the Signer will use depends on his/her *perception* of the duration or frequency of that event. (This is similar to the way the Signer's *perspective* influences the choice of classifiers.) Non-manual signals frequently occur with verbs (or predicate adjectives) that have been modulated to show "temporal aspect". However, there are logical restrictions on which signals can occur with which modulations.

Finally, the four modulations described in these texts are not the only modulations for temporal aspect that occur in ASL. Interaction with native Deaf Signers will likely expose you to additional ways through which Signers communicate their perceptions of the temporal aspect of an event.

G. Text Analysis

$$\overline{}^{\text{co}}\qquad\overline{}^{\text{t}}\qquad\overline{}^{\text{q}}$$

Pat$_1$: "UMMM" + KNOW-THAT YOU △ , BECOME-SICK, KNOW-THAT YOU

- △

    While name signs are frequently derived from some phys-ical characteristic of the individual or are related to the individual's English name, there are less personal ways in which deaf children have been assigned name signs. For example, it is reported that deaf students in some oral programs in this country and in England were assigned name signs which corresponded to their locker numbers or coat hook numbers. Thus, deaf children would use these numbers to refer to each other.

- **BECOME-SICK**

    As described in the *General Discussion* section above, signs glossed as **SICK, SILLY, FRUSTRATED, WRONG,** etc., are usually thought of as "adjectives". However, in a sentence like the one above, the adjective also includes the meaning of the verb 'to become'. Thus, it seems more appropriate to gloss this *predicate adjective* as **BECOME-SICK.**

Lee$_1$:   INDEX-*lf* TEND-TO BE-SICK*"over time"*

- **INDEX-*lf***

    Notice that since Pat did not assign a location to △ in Pat$_1$, Lee now establishes a location with this sign—Lee's left and Pat's right.

- **BE-SICK***"over time"*

    This is an example of a predicate adjective occurring with the *"over time"* modulation. This modulation of the sign **BE-SICK** conveys the meaning 'characteristically sick'.

<u>   q nod</u>

Pat₃: **YOU KNOW INDEX**-*rt* **WORK #VR INDEX**-*rt,*

ONE-WEEK-PAST SOMETHING IMPORTANT,

                                 <u>'intently'</u>

INDEX-*rt* ⚠ **INDEX**-*rt* **WORK**"over time" **ALL-WEEK,**

                                                                   <u>sta</u>

ALL-DAY ALL-NIGHT ALL-DAY ALL-NIGHT WORK"over & over again",

                          <u>t</u>

FEW-DAY-PAST, BECOME-SERIOUSLY-ILL THROW-*rt* **HOSPITAL**

- **INDEX**-*rt*

  Notice that Pat uses the spatial location assigned to ⚠ by Lee.

- **#VR**

  This is another fingerspelled loan sign. Notice that when spelling this loan sign, the palm of the hand faces the Signer during the '**V**' and then twists out to face the Addressee for the '**R**'.

                 <u>'intently'</u>
- **WORK**"*over time*"

  The modulation "*over time*" has been described in Units 17 and 26. Notice that the Signer's facial behavior conveys the meaning 'intently'. It is common for a non-manual adverb to occur with a sign that has a modulation for temporal aspect.

- **ALL-DAY ALL-NIGHT**

  Notice that these two signs are produced in such a way that they look like a single sign. When used together like this, they mean something like 'around the clock'.

                       <u>sta</u>
- **WORK**"*over & over again*"

  Notice the non-manual '*sta*' signal—which often occurs with the "*over & over again*" modulation. It conveys the meanings 'hard'; 'too much'; or 'over and over again'. (This signal also occurred with three of the verbs in Lee's fourth turn in Unit 13.) See how the signal involves a tense opening and closing of the mouth in the photos below.

'sta'

<pre>
                                   (gaze lf, lean lf   ) 'intently'
Pat₄: (2h)"WELL",   DOCTOR   (2h)SEARCH-body(lf)"over time"
</pre>

<pre>
       (body shift rt, gaze lf 'anxiously')   neg
  ⚠ WAIT-lf"long time",   NOT-YET   doctor(lf)-INFORM-john(rt)
</pre>

- **DOCTOR**

  This is an *initialized* sign—a sign which has been influenced by English. The handshape in this sign is the same as the **'D'** handshape in the manual alphabet. Unit 4 illustrates how some Signers will use the older and newer forms of the sign **DOCTOR** within the same conversation.

(gaze lf, lean lf   ) 'intently'
- (2h)**SEARCH**-body(lf)"over time"

  Notice that the Signer *role plays* the doctor who examined ⚠ by gazing left and leaning left while taking on the facial behaviors of the doctor.

(body shift rt, gaze lf 'anxiously')
- ⚠ **WAIT**-lf"long time"

  Then, by a body shift to the right, the Signer role plays ⚠ who looks toward the location of the doctor (left) while 'anxiously waiting' to hear the results. Notice also that Pat portrays ⚠ as waiting for a "*long time*". This modulation was described in Units 8 and 17 and in this unit.

<pre>
                                      br   sta
Pat₅: "WELL" UP-TIL-NOW THREE-DAY, WIFE (2h)CRY"long time",

                                    nodding
         ME FEEL BREAK-DOWN FEEL ME
</pre>

                           br
- **THREE-DAY**

    Notice how this time sign indicates a specific number of 'days' by incorporating the handshape for the number '3' into the sign.

                                sta
- **(2h)CRY**"long time"

    Notice how the non-manual 'sta' signal conveys the meanings 'hard' or 'over and over again' while the modulation shows that the Signer feels the event lasted for a 'long time'.

- **BREAK-DOWN**

    When this sign is used in reference to human beings (as opposed to machines as in Unit 21) it can mean a physical, mental, or emotional breakdown.

                  nodding
- **FEEL ME**

    Notice how the 'nodding' signal emphasizes that the Signer really does feel the wife will have a breakdown.

<pre>
                  (gaze lf)   wh-q   (br squint)q
Lee₅: WHY NOT US-TWO FROM-here-GO-TO-lf HOSPITAL (2h)NOW, WANTwg
</pre>

- **WHY NOT**

    This is another example of two signs which are produced in such a way that they look like a single sign. There are a number of other signs like this in which one of the signs expresses negation. (See the *General Discussion* section in Unit 19.)

- **US-TWO**

  In producing this sign, Signers will either use the hand-shape shown on the left or its variant on the right.

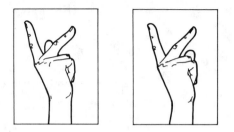

<u>(br squint)q</u>
- **WANTwg**

  Notice how the 'wiggling' movement of the fingers extends or prolongs the sign—which frequently happens to the last sign in a question (see Units 1 and 10).

Pat₆: <u>puff.cheeks+nodding</u>
YES++

  <u>puff.cheeks+ nodding</u>
- **YES++**

  Notice how these two combined non-manual signals convey the meanings 'very much so' and 'definitely'.

H. Sample Drills

1. <u>t</u>
△,   **INDEX-*rt***   **TEND-TO**   <u>   mm   </u>
BE-SICK"*over time*"

             |

             <u>puff.cheeks</u>
BECOME-SICK"*regularly*"

             |

             <u>tight lips</u>
j-**TEASE**-*me*"*over time*"

             |

             <u>th</u>
BE-SICK"*long time*"

             |

             <u>sta</u>
BECOME-SICK"*over & over again*"

             |

             <u>th</u>
BE-WRONG"*over time*"

             |

             <u>th</u>
(2h)**BE-SILLY** "*long time*"

             |

             <u>mm</u>
BE-SICK"*over time*"

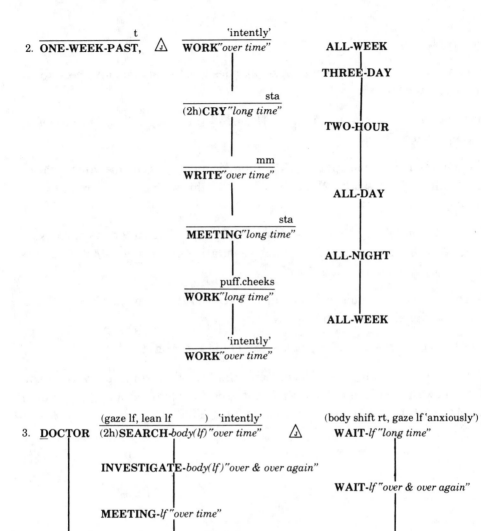

2. $\overline{\text{ONE-WEEK-PAST,}}^{\text{t}}$ ⚠ $\overline{\textbf{WORK}''\textit{over time}''}^{\text{'intently'}}$ **ALL-WEEK**

                                                                                     THREE-DAY

                            $\overline{\text{(2h)}\textbf{CRY}''\textit{long time}''}^{\text{sta}}$

                                                                                     TWO-HOUR

                            $\overline{\textbf{WRITE}''\textit{over time}''}^{\text{mm}}$

                                                                                     ALL-DAY

                            $\overline{\textbf{MEETING}''\textit{long time}''}^{\text{sta}}$

                                                                                     ALL-NIGHT

                            $\overline{\textbf{WORK}''\textit{long time}''}^{\text{puff.cheeks}}$

                                                                                     ALL-WEEK

                            $\overline{\textbf{WORK}''\textit{over time}''}^{\text{'intently'}}$

3. $\underline{\text{D}}$**OCTOR** $\overline{\text{(2h)}\textbf{SEARCH-}\textit{body(lf)}''\textit{over time}''}^{\text{(gaze lf, lean lf}\qquad\text{) 'intently'}}$ ⚠ $\overline{\textbf{WAIT-}\textit{lf}''\textit{long time}''}^{\text{(body shift rt, gaze lf 'anxiously')}}$

         INVESTIGATE-\textit{body(lf)}''\textit{over \& over again}''   **WAIT-**\textit{lf}''\textit{over \& over again}''

         MEETING-\textit{lf}''\textit{over time}''

TEACH ◡ **AGENT**   **PLAY-**\textit{lf}''\textit{over time}''

                            $\overline{\textit{teacher-}\textbf{TEACH-}\textit{j}''\textit{regularly}''}^{\text{mm}}$ $\overline{\textit{j-}\textbf{LOOK-AT-}\textit{teacher}''\textit{over time}''}^{\text{'intently'}}$

         WRITE''\textit{over time}''

                                                                                     $\overline{\textbf{READ-}''\textit{over time}''}^{\text{'intently'}}$

$\underline{\text{D}}$**OCTOR**

                                                                                     WAIT-\textit{lf}''\textit{long time}''

                   (2h)**SEARCH-**\textit{body(lf)}''\textit{over time}''

I. Video Notes

If you have access to the videotape package designed to accompany these texts, you will notice the following:

- How Pat shakes her index finger (**"UMMM"+**) to get Lee's attention before beginning to converse.

- The modulation of the sign **BE-SICK** (Lee$_1$) which gives the meaning 'characteristically sick' or 'sickly'. Notice how Lee does this with a small, circular wrist movement.

- The *"over time"*, *"long time"*, and *"over & over again"* modulations of the sign **WORK.** Also compare the *"long time"* modulation of the sign **WAIT** with the same modulation of the sign **CRY.**

- Compare the *'sta'* signals which occur in Pat$_3$ and Pat$_4$. Notice which modulations this signal occurs with.

- How Lee 'holds' the **INDEX**-*lf* at the end of his question (Lee$_3$).

- The way Pat role plays the 'doctor' and the 'friend' during her fourth turn. Notice how she switches out of the role of the doctor while signing ⚠ and then out of the role of the friend while signing **NOT-YET,** etc.

Unit 27

Distributional Aspect

A. Synopsis

Pat and Lee meet during their coffee break. Pat asks Lee where s/he has been for the past week. Lee explains that s/he was called for jury duty. During the selection process, Lee was the only Deaf person in a group of fifty or so. It was really fascinating. The lawyer first passed out a sheet of paper for names, addresses, etc. Then the lawyer asked whether people had read the newspaper, watched TV, etc., because if they had, they couldn't serve on the jury. People who said they had were eliminated. Lee wasn't eliminated because s/he hasn't read the paper for a good while. So s/he was left in the remaining group of 15.

B. Cultural Information: Deaf People and Jury Duty

It is generally true that Deaf people rarely, if ever, receive notices to report for jury duty. In fact, most states have laws which specifically prohibit the names of Deaf people from being included in the "jury pool". (The jury pool is a list of people's names who can be called for jury duty if the need arises.) The rationale that is most often used to exclude Deaf individuals is that the inability to *hear* testimony prevents them from being competent jurors.

However, with the signing of Section 504 of the Rehabilitation Act of 1973, Deaf people are demanding their right to participate more fully and equally in all aspects of American society. During the past few years, individuals and groups have begun to organize efforts to change state laws which prohibit Deaf people from being called for jury duty. The focus of these efforts is simply to allow Deaf individuals to be included in the jury pool. Since any potential juror can be challenged and not chosen for jury duty, being included in the jury pool does not mean that a person will be selected to serve on a jury. However, at least Deaf people would not be automatically excluded simply because they cannot hear.

During the past few years, a few Deaf individuals have served on juries. These individuals live in states which do not automatically exclude Deaf people from jury duty. In the state of Washington, a Deaf man served on a jury in a criminal case and, reportedly, was the first Deaf juror to serve on a criminal trial in this country. Experiences and precedents such as this one help support and motivate efforts to change state laws which deny Deaf people the right to serve on juries. Apart from the increasing awareness that Deaf people can be effective jurors, there is the recognition that automatically excluding any group from jury duty prevents a fair cross-section of the community from being represented. For further information about legal action being taken to assure that the rights of Deaf people are not violated, contact: The National Center for Law and the Deaf, Gallaudet College, 7th Street and Florida Avenue, N.E., Washington, D.C. 20002.

C. Dialogue

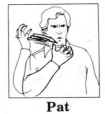

Pat

Pat₁: "HI" (2h)"WELL" ONE-WEEK-PAST <u>NOT○HERE WORK,</u>^{neg} <u>YOU SICK YOU</u>^q

Pat₂: <u>neg('not understand')</u>   <u>#DO-DO YOU,</u>^{wh-q} <u>J-U-R-Y</u>^q

Pat₃: YOU HAVE INTERPRET○AGENT <u>YOU</u>^q

Pat₄: FOR-FOR ASK-TO-*people"each"* <u>"WHAT"</u>^{wh-q}

Pat₅: <u>ELIMINATE YOU</u>^q

Pat₆: <u>OH-I-SEE</u>^{nodding}

Lee

Lee₁:
    <u>neg   </u>   <u>(gaze lf   )</u>
       ME STUCK,   *lf*-SUMMON-*me* (2h)GO-TO-*lf* COURT, "WOW"

Lee₂:
    <u>nod   </u>   <u>(gaze lf   )</u>
  RIGHT J-U-R-Y,   (2h)alt.SELECT-*people(lf)"spec"* (2h)C-CL-*lf*'group' THEREABOUTS-*lf* FIFTY++,
                                       (hold lf C-CL) ————————————————————→

  (lean,gaze lf) (lean rt,gaze lf) (lean,gaze lf) (lean rt,gaze lf)
   MAN-*lf*,   WOMAN,   BLACK,   WHITE-FACED, ONLY-ONE-*me* DEAF

Lee₃:
    <u>nod </u> <u>(gaze lf   )</u> <u>puff.cheeks</u>   <u>t</u>
  YES++ FASCINATINGwg "WOW"++, INDEX-*lf thumb+* LAW AGENT,

  <u>(gaze lf   )</u>
  lawyer-GIVE-TO-*people(lf)"each"* (2h)1_outline-CL'rectangular paper',

  <u>(gaze lf   )</u>   <u>nod   </u><u>t</u> <u>(gaze down,lf   )</u>
  NAME ADDRESS VARIOUS-THINGS, INDEX-*lf index+*, (2h)alt.*lawyer*-ASK-TO-*people(lf)"spec"*

  <u>(gaze down,lf   )</u> (<u>puff.cheeks)q</u>
  FINISH-*lf* READ-*paper-lf* NEWSPAPER-*lf*, LOOK-AT-*lf+* # TV-*lf+*, VARIOUS-THINGS

Lee₄:
         <u>(nod)br</u>   <u>(gaze lf   )</u>
  SUPPOSE FINISH*-*lf* READ-*paper-lf* NEWSPAPER-*lf*, LOOK-AT-*lf* #TV+,

                                          <u>neg</u>
  KNOW+ PROBLEM SITUATION, <u>CAN'T J-U-R-Y CAN'T,</u> DOESN'T-MATTER,

  (gaze down, lf   ) <u>t</u> (body lean lf;gaze up,lf)puff.cheeks+nodding
  (2h)alt.*lawyer*-ASK-TO-*people"spec"*, PEOPLE, (2h)alt."spec"*people*-SAY-#YES-TO-*lawyer*,

  (gaze down, lf   )
  (2h)alt.*lawyer*-INDEX-*people"spec"* (2h)alt.*lawyer*-ELIMINATE-*people"spec"*

Lee₅:
    <u>neg</u> <u>   t</u>
  ME, READ-*paper* NEWSPAPER, BEHIND* "WOW"+,

  <u>(gaze lf   )t</u> (gaze lf   ) <u>rhet.q</u>
  (2h)C-CL'relatively large group', (2h)L:-CL'class dwindle in size', LEAVE-IT-*lf*, FIFTEEN+

D. Key Illustrations

Pat

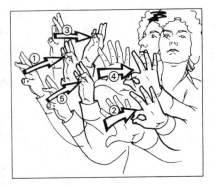

neg
———
NOT⏜HERE

wh-q
———
DO-DO

Lee

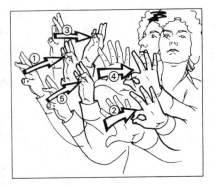

(2h)alt.SELECT-*lf* "spec"

ONLY-ONE-*me*

FASCINATING*wg*

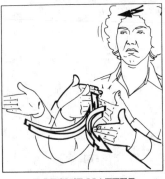

DOESN'T-MATTER
(or ANYWAY)

(2h)alt."spec"-SAY-# YES-TO-*lawyer*

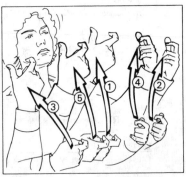

(2h)alt.*lawyer*-ELIMINATE-"spec"

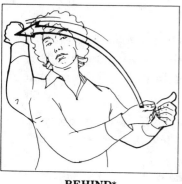

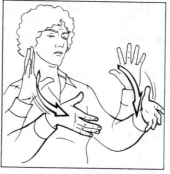

BEHIND*   (2h)C-CL'relatively large group'   (2h)L:-CL'group dwindle in size'

E. Supplementary Illustrations

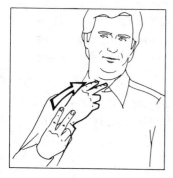

STUCK   *rt*-SUMMON-*me*   *lawyer*-GIVE-TO-*"each"*

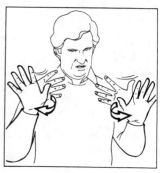

(2h)1outline-CL'rectangular'   (2h)alt.*lawyer*-ASK-TO-*"spec"*   **FINISH***

F. General Discussion: Distributional Aspect

The two previous discussions of distributional aspect (Units 9 and 18) presented four modulations that indicate how an action is 'distributed'. These four modulations are described below. Their approximate meaning is given in italics, followed by a description of the movement of each modulation.

(a) *'to all in a group'*: This is made with a 'sweep' of the hand in an arc on a horizontal plane. The Signer's eyes/head tend to follow the 'sweep'. We call this modulation *"all"*.

(b) *'to or from each in a group'*: This modulation is made with repeated, separate productions of the verb in an arc. The Signer's eyes/head tend to follow each production along the arc. We call this modulation *"each"*.

(c) *'to or from specified individuals (some/many, usually not all)'*: This modulation is made with repeated productions of the verb, with both hands alternating and moving toward or from several different points in space (not in serial order). The Signer's eyes/head tend to move back and forth with each production, and there is frequently some kind of repeated opening and closing of the mouth (often releasing air from the mouth with each production). We call this modulation *"spec"*.

(d) *'to or from un-specified individuals (some/many, but not all)'*: This modulation is made with repeated productions of the verb, with both hands alternating in a somewhat circular manner. The Signer's eyes/head tend not to focus on any specific point, but the head 'bobs' with each production of the verb. Sometimes the head is bent forward with the eyes partially or fully closed—which shows a lack of attention to any specific individuals. Sometimes the cheeks are 'puffed', releasing air. We call this modulation *"unspec"*.

These four modulations are illustrated below with the directional verbs ___-**GIVE-TO-**___ and ___-**ASK-TO-**___. Note the movement of the hands and of the eyes and head with each modulation.

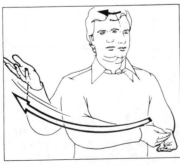

me-**GIVE-TO-**"*all*"

me-**ASK-TO-**"*all*"

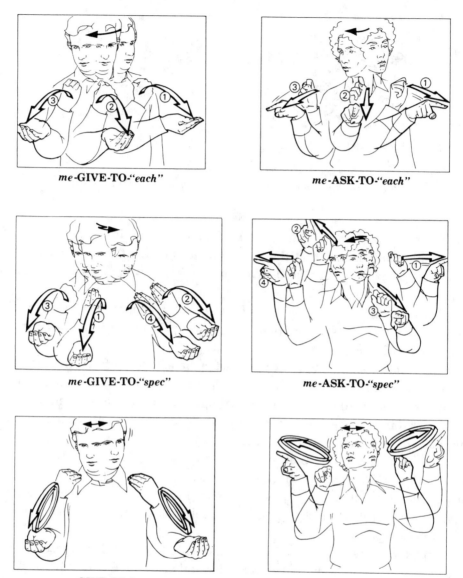

me-GIVE-TO-*"each"*   *me*-ASK-TO-*"each"*

me-GIVE-TO-*"spec"*   *me*-ASK-TO-*"spec"*

me-GIVE-TO-*"unspec"*   *me*-ASK-TO-*"unspec"*

In the illustrations above, notice how each of them indicates that the object is plural (and more than two). Similarly, the *"each"*, *"spec"*, and *"unspec"* modulations can indicate that the subject is plural. This is seen in the dialogue in this unit where 'various specific individuals say "yes" to the lawyer'. This was also seen in Unit 9 where 'various unspecified individuals asked questions to the man' and in Unit 18 where 'various unspecified deaf individuals sent letters to the company (role played by the Signer)'.

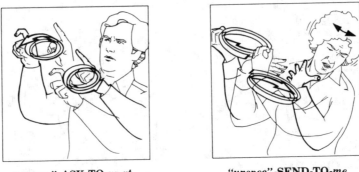

"unspec"-ASK-TO-up,rt   "unspec"-SEND-TO-me

Recall how these four modulations differ from each other in their meanings. The "all" modulation indicates that the action happens to all of the individuals but it doesn't specify exactly how the distribution occurs. It's like saying 'it happened to them'.

The "each" modulation also indicates that the action happens to all of the individuals. But it additionally specifies that the action happens to (or from) each person or thing individually.

The "spec" modulation indicates that an action happens to (or from) various specific people or things individually. However, unlike the "each" modulation, it does not generally happen to all of the people or things. It also does not happen to them in serial order. Instead, the "spec" modulation indicates that the action happens with 'this one here' and then 'that one over there', etc.

The "unspec" modulation indicates that an action happens to (or from) various people or things. It also shows that the action does not happen to all of the people or things. However, in this case, the Signer does not focus on specific individuals; they remain un-specified—like saying 'lots of people asked her questions' or 'he sent letters to lots of people'.

In summary, Signers choose to use a modulation like one of those described above when they want to give more detailed information about the 'distribution' of an action. They can simply state that the action happened to all the members of a group or say that it involved each individual or thing in serial order, various specific individuals or things in non-serial order, or many un-specified individuals or things in non-serial order.

However, the four modulations described in these texts are probably not the only modulations for distributional aspect that occur in ASL. Interaction with native Deaf Signers will likely expose you to additional ways in which Signers communicate information about the 'distribution' of an action.

G. Text Analysis

<u> neg </u>   (gaze lf   )

Lee₁: ME   STUCK,   *lf*-SUMMON-*me*   (2h)GO-TO-*lf*   COURT,   "WOW"

- <u>neg</u>

> Notice that Lee responds to Pat's "yes-no" question by using the *'neg'* signal and then explains why s/he wasn't at work last week.

    (gaze lf   )

- *lf*-SUMMON-*me*   (2h)**GO-TO**-*lf*

> Notice that ____-**SUMMON**-____ is a directional verb which can indicate its subject and object. However, in this case, the subject of the verb is not explicit. This is like saying, in English, "They called me into court" or "I was called into court".
>
> However, notice how the two verbs in this sentence 'agree with' each other, showing that the location to Lee's left represents the 'court'.

  <u> nod </u>   (gaze lf   )

ee₂: RIGHT   J-U-R-Y,   (2h)alt.**SELECT**-*people(lf)*"*spec*"   (2h)**C-CL**-*lf*'group'   **THEREABOUTS**-*lf*   **FIFTY++**,

                                                (hold lf C-CL) ——————————————→

(lean,gaze lf)   (lean rt,gaze lf)   (lean,gaze lf)   (lean rt,gaze lf)

   MAN-*lf,*   WOMAN,   BLACK,   WHITE-FACED,   ONLY-ONE-*me*   DEAF

- (2h)alt.**SELECT**-*people(lf)*"*spec*"

> Notice that this verb occurs with the "*spec*" modulation which was discussed in Units 18 and 27. The information which is conveyed is that specific people were selected one-by-one.

- (2h)**C-CL**-*lf*'group'   **THEREABOUTS**-*lf*   **FIFTY++**
  (hold lf C-CL) ——————————————→

> Notice that the sign which is often glossed as **CLASS** is actually a classifier. It is frequently used for setting up groups in different spatial locations and can also be moved as a verb.
>
> Notice how Lee 'holds' the group while describing how many people were in it and how the sign **THEREABOUTS**-*lf* 'agrees with' the location of the group.

  (lean,gaze lf)   (lean rt,gaze lf)   (lean,gaze lf)   (lean rt,gaze lf)

-    MAN-*lf*   WOMAN   BLACK   WHITE-FACED

> Notice the Signer alternately leans to the left and to the right while listing the various 'types' of people in the group—all the while maintaining gaze toward the group s/he is describing.
>
> The sign **WHITE-FACED** is sometimes glossed as **PALE** or **PALE-FACE** because it can also be used to describe a person's appearance when s/he is frightened or sick.

- **ONLY-ONE**-*me*

    This sign can be moved toward a particular location to show who or what it refers to. Note the difference between the sign **ONLY-ONE**-*me* (illustrated above) and the sign **ONLY-ONE**-*you* illustrated here.

ONE-ONE-*you*

<pre>
          nod   (gaze lf   ) puff.cheeks   t
Lee₃: YES++ FASCINATINGwg "WOW"++, INDEX-lf thumb+   LAW   AGENT,

        (gaze lf   )
        lawyer-GIVE-TO-people(lf)"each"   (2h)1outline-CL'rectangular paper',

        (gaze lf   )   nod   t   (gaze down,lf   )
        NAME ADDRESS VARIOUS-THINGS, INDEX-lf index+, (2h)alt.lawyer-ASK-TO-people(lf)"spec"

        (gaze down,lf   ) (puff.cheeks)q
        FINISH-lf READ-paper-lf NEWSPAPER-lf, LOOK-AT-lf+ #TV-lf+, VARIOUS-THINGS
</pre>

-    (gaze lf   )
  FASCINATINGwg

    This sign can move toward a particular location, thus indicating the person or thing that is 'fascinating' to the Signer (e.g. one could sign **FASCINATING**wg-*lf* or **FASCINATING**wg-*rt*).

- **INDEX**-*lf thumb*+

    See the *General Discussion* section in Unit 21 and the *Text Analysis* section of Unit 25 for information about this type of listing or counting using the fingers of the passive hand. Here Lee is listing the events that happened.

- *lawyer*-**GIVE-TO**-*people(lf)"each"*

    Notice how the *"each"* modulation with this directional verb indicates that the same action ('giving') occurred again and again, each time to a different person. The action proceeded in an orderly fashion and each person in the group was given a copy of the form.

- (2h)**1**_{outline}**-CL**'rectangular paper'

    This classifier basically 'outlines' or 'traces' the shape of the referent. Other classifiers that can function this way are the **5**_{outline}**-CL** and **B**_{outline}**-CL.** Notice this 'outlining' in the following illustrations.

1_{outline}**-CL**'circular'   (2h)**B**_{outline}**-CL**-*cntr*'hill'

- (2h)alt.*lawyer*-**ASK-TO**-*people(lf)* "*spec*"

    In the illustration above, notice how the Signer's gaze and head movement clearly show the lawyer's focus on specific individuals. This "*spec*" modulation is described in the *General Discussion* section of this Unit and Unit 18.

Pat₄:
<u>   wh-q   </u>
FOR-FOR   ASK-TO-*people*"*each*"   "**WHAT**"

- **ASK-TO**-*people*"*each*"

    Here Pat is focusing on those individuals who were questioned by the lawyer and asks why 'each of them' was questioned.

Lee₄:
<u>   (nod)br   </u>   <u>(gaze lf   )</u>
SUPPOSE   FINISH*-*lf*   **READ**-*paper-lf*   **NEWSPAPER**-*lf*,   **LOOK-AT**-*lf*   **# TV+** ,

                                              <u>neg   </u>
KNOW+   PROBLEM   SITUATION,   CAN'T   J-U-R-Y   CAN'T,   DOESN'T-MATTER,

(gaze down,lf   )   <u>   t</u> (body lean lf;gaze up,lf)puff.cheeks+nodding
(2h)alt*lawyer*-**ASK-TO**-*people*"*spec*",   **PEOPLE**,   (2h)alt."*spec*"*people*-**SAY-#YES-TO**-*lawyer*,

(gaze down,lf   )   )
(2h)alt*lawyer*-**INDEX**-*people*"*spec*"   (2h)alt*lawyer*-**ELIMINATE**-*people*"*spec*"

<u>   neg   </u>
- **CAN'T   J-U-R-Y   CAN'T**

    Notice the repetition of the negation sign **CAN'T.** Negation signs can occur before a verb or at the end of a sentence (which seems to emphasize the sign.) However, negation signs can also be repeated—i.e. signed before the verb and at the end of the sentence. This also emphasizes the negation.

- **DOESN'T-MATTER**

    Here this sign (also sometimes glossed as **ANYWAY**) is used to show that Lee is finished responding to Pat's question and wants to continue describing what happened.

(body lean lf;gaze up,lf)puff.cheeks+ nodding
- (2h)alt.*"spec"people*-**SAY-# YES-TO-***lawyer*

    Notice that the *"spec"* modulation is used here with the directional verb_____-**SAY-# YES-TO-**_____. This means that, one-by-one, various people said "yes" to the lawyer. Thus, the subject of the verb is plural (people) but the object is singular (lawyer). Compare this verb with the verb (2h)alt.*lawyer*-**ASK-TO**-*people"spec"* (Lee₄) where the subject is singular (lawyer) and the object is plural (people).

    Notice also how the non-manual signal *'puff.cheeks'* conveys the information that 'a lot' of people said "yes".

- (2h)alt.*lawyer*-**ELIMINATE**-*people"spec"*

    The sign **ELIMINATE-**____ can be produced at or toward a specific location to indicate who or what is 'eliminated'. For example, it is sometimes used when the fingers of the non-dominant hand serve as locations (as in Lee₃ in this unit, or Lee₂ in Unit 25). Thus, a Signer might produce a sentence such as:

    CAN INDEX-*lf thumb* **SKI, INDEX-***lf index*

    neg

    WALK, WRONG ELIMINATE-*ski*

neg   t
Lee₅: **ME,** **READ-***paper* **NEWSPAPER,** **BEHIND*** **"WOW"+,**

(gaze lf   )t   (gaze lf   )   rhet.q
(2h)**C-CL**'relatively large group', (2h)**L:-CL**'class dwindle in size', **LEAVE-IT-***lf,* **FIFTEEN+**

           (gaze lf   )t
- (2h)**C-CL**'relatively large group'

    The (2h)**C-CL** classifier can be used to indicate either a relatively large group or a relatively small group. Compare the illustration of (2h)**C-CL**'relatively large group' with the sign illustrated below.

(2h)C-CL'relatively small group'

                   rhet.q
- **LEAVE-IT-*lf***

> Notice the non-manual signal *'rhet.q'*. This would be comparable to saying, in English, "And how many were left? Fifteen". The specific behaviors in this signal are described in Units 10 and 19.

H. Sample Drills

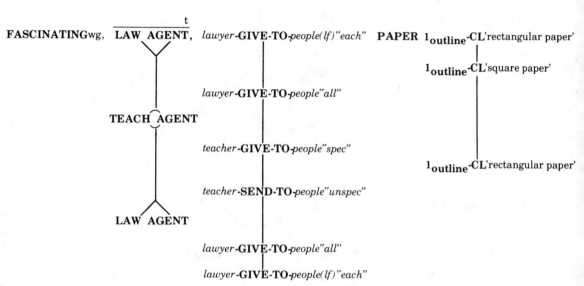

                                  t
FASCINATINGwg, LAW AGENT, *lawyer*-**GIVE-TO**-*people(lf)"each"* PAPER 1_{outline}-**CL**'rectangular paper'

                                                1_{outline}-**CL**'square paper'

                          lawyer-**GIVE-TO**-*people"all"*

TEACH AGENT

                          teacher-**GIVE-TO**-*people"spec"*   1_{outline}-**CL**'rectangular paper'

                          teacher-**SEND-TO**-*people"unspec"*

LAW AGENT

                          lawyer-**GIVE-TO**-*people"all"*

                          lawyer-**GIVE-TO**-*people(lf)"each"*

                                             q   t   puff.cheeks
(2h)alt.*me*-**ASK-TO**-*people"spec"* **LOOK-AT**-*lf* #TV+, PEOPLE, (2h)alt.*"spec"people*-**SAY-#YES-TO**-*me*

                                                      (2h)alt.*"spec"people*-**SAY-#NO-TO**-*me*

    me-**ASK-TO**-*people"each"*

                                                        "each"-**SAY-#YES-TO**-*me*

    me-**ASK-TO**-*people"all"*

                                                    (2h)alt.*"spec"people*-**SAY-#NO-TO**-*me*

    me-**ASK-TO**-*people"spec"*

                                                   (2h)alt.*"spec"people*-**SAY-#YES-TO**-*me*

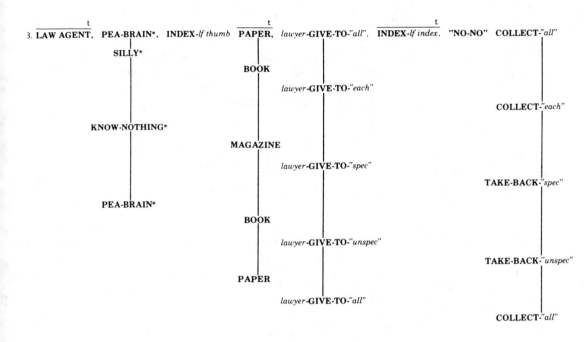

3. LAW AGENT, PEA-BRAIN*, INDEX-*lf thumb* PAPER, *lawyer*-GIVE-TO-"all", INDEX-*lf index*, "NO-NO" COLLECT-"all"

I. Video Notes

If you have access to the videotape package designed to accompany these texts, you will notice the following:

- The difference between the movement of the sign **SICK** (a repeated form of **BE-SICK**) in Pat_1 and the movement of the sign **BECOME-SICK** in Pat_1 (Unit 26).

- In Lee_3, Lee's mouth movement with each production of the sign ____-**GIVE-TO**-___ (which has the *"each"* modulation). Also notice that the sign is made here with an 'X' handshape (rather than the handshape shown in the illustration).

- How Lee changes his body position when explaining what the 'lawyer' did (give out papers, ask questions, eliminate people) as opposed to what the 'people' did (say "yes" to the lawyer). Lee gazes downward and to the left when describing the lawyer's actions. When describing the people's response, he leans his body and head to the left—'into' the location of the people; 'from' that location, he responds.

- How Lee actually *role plays* the lawyer during the question at the end of his third turn.

Video Package Notes:

If you have access to the videotape package designed to accompany these texts, you will see the following stories, poems, and narrative descriptions which appear after dialogues 19-27.

The Blackout Blues — Gilbert C. Eastman
These three short stories are all true. They vividly portray the Signer's experiences during the blackout drills of World War II. Notice the classifier handshapes he uses throughout the stories and how he "role plays" different characters.

Home Is Where Your Hands Are — M.J. Bienvenu
This true story is about the Signer's grandfather and his first experiences at a school for deaf children. Notice how she "role plays" the grandfather as a child and how she describes the location of the school and the train journey.

Mother Knows Best — Nathie Couthen
Notice how the Signer shifts her body and facial expressions to "role play" the mother and daughter in this amusing story. Notice also the Signer's different signing style when she portrays the daughter.

Let Your Fingers Do The Talking — M.J. Bienvenu
This true story describes one of the Signer's experiences in a school which advocated the use of fingerspelling as the primary means of communication with students. Notice her use of directional verbs — and her attitude toward having to fingerspell all day at school!

Grand Canyon Sunset — Larry Berke
In this very graphic description of a daredevilish dream and misadventure, notice the extensive use of classifier handshapes and how much information they convey. Notice also how the Signer uses the lower central portion of the signing space to give a sense of height and distance.

The Harmfulness of Tobacco — An Excerpt — Pat Graybill
Pat Graybill is a former member of NTD. This is an excerpt from a longer piece by Chekhov which Pat translated and performed with NTD. Notice the obvious theatrical style of the Signer in assuming the role of the narrator and his wife.

Sign Is Like A Tree — Ellz Lentz
This is an original poem created by Ella Lentz. Notice that repeatedly throughout the poem, she uses signs which are similar in handshape (visual "rhyme"?). The non-dominant hand is also used quite differently than it is used in normal conversation. More important than the form of the poem, however, is the message of the poem.

In Motion — Larry Berke
This story is told almost exclusively with classifiers. It is part of a much longer (15-20 minute) story which the Signer has developed. In all languages there are certain uses of the language which defy complete interpretation (e.g. English puns). This is such a case in ASL!

INDEX OF ILLUSTRATIONS

The following is a list of all of the sign illustrations in this text. The illustrations in each unit are listed alphabetically according to their glosses. In cases where the illustration appears in more than one unit, those units are listed on the right.

163

EVERY-OTHER-MONDAY

EVERY-TWO-YEAR

FEW-DAY-FUTURE

FEW-DAY-PAST . . . 23

(2h)# FIX-*arc*

FOR-MONTHS-AND-MONTHS

FOR-WEEKS-AND-WEEKS

FROM-NOW-ON

KNOW-THAT . . . 19

LONG-TIME-PAST . . . 22

MEETING

(2h)NONE

NONE

NONE (colloquial)

NONE (emphatic)

ONE-MONTH

ONE-YEAR-FUTURE

POSTPONE*"long time"*

RECENT

SAME-OLD-THING

SOMETIME-IN-THE-AFTERNOON

SOMETIME-IN-THE-MORNING

THREE-MONTH

THREE-O'CLOCK

TRAVEL-AROUND

TWO-WEEK . . . 22

TWO-WEEK-FUTURE

TWO-WEEK-PAST . . . 25

UP-TIL-NOW . . . 22

WANT

WANTwg

WILL

Unit 21
Pronominalization

BREAK-DOWN . . . 26

OH-I-SEE

OURSELVES

POSS+ -*rt*

POSS-*rt*+ + 'characteristically'

QM

QMwg

REALLY-ADEPT . . . 23

SILLY*

SOMEONE-*rt* . . . 19

SUPPOSE . . . 25

TEND-TO-*rt* . . . 26

TEND-TO‿POSS-*rt*

THAT-ONE‿POSS-*rt*

THAT-ONE-*rt* . . . 24

WE

you-INFORM-*rt*

you-TTY-CALL-TO-*rt* . . . 22

YOUR (plural)

YOUR ⟷ POSS-*rt*

Unit 22
Subjects and Objects

BAWL-EYES-OUT

they-CLASH-WITH-*"each other"*+*"regularly"*

CONSCIENCE+

they-CORRESPOND-WITH-*"each other"*

Unit 23
Classifiers

Unit 24
Locatives

#HURT-*lf shoulder*

PURPLE 5:-**CL**'bruise on cheek'

THAT-ONE-*rt* . . . 21

THEREABOUTS . . . 22

WATER (2h)**L**:-**CL@***lf* 'lake'

(2h)**"WHAT"**

WOW

(2h)alt.**C-CL**'on wall'

(2h)**A-CL**"*sweep in rows*"-'trophies' . . . 25

(2h)alt.**V-CL**'on floor'

(2h)**4-CL**-*up,lf* 'in a line facing Signer'

A-CL-*rt*'trophy'
C-CL@*rt*'cup behind trophy'

B-CL-*cntr*'front face of lake'
B-CL-*cntr*'hilltop'

B-CL-*rt*'hill next to lake'
L:-CL-*lf* 'lake'

C-CL-*rt* ⎫ 'cup on table is
B↑-CL-*rt* ⎭ turned on its side'

V:-CL-*rt*
1-CL'swerve to lf to miss rabbit'

V-CL@*cntr*'stand on hill'
B-CL-*cntr*'hilltop'

V:-CL@*rt,out* ⎫ 'sit facing
V:-CL@*rt,in* ⎭ each other'

V-CL-*lf* 'fall over fence'
4-CL-*lf* 'fence'

1-CL-*cntr*'ski down hill, weaving
side to side'

*3→***CL**-*rt*'car'
RED **BURST-OF**-*light*

*3→***CL**-*rt*'car stopped'
*3→***CL**'car from lf smash into lf rear'

(2h)**4-CL**-*lf* 'fence on side of hill'
TREE-*rt,upward-arc*'trees on side of hill'

5:↓ -CL-*rt,cntr*
INDEX-*lf,cntr* . . . 23

5:↓ -CL-*rt*'school'
B-CL'road near school' . . . 23

Unit 25
Pluralization

ASSEMBLE-TO-*cntr*

COLLECT"*all*"

COLLECT"*each*"

DIFFERENT+++-*arc*

#DO-DO . . . 20, 27

DON'T-CARE

KNOW-NOTHING

LIST-OF-ITEMS

LUCKY **YOU**

NOT-YET

NOTICE-TO-*rt*

PERFECT

RELIEVED

SEVERAL

"SO-SO"

SPECIALTY-FIELD

SUPPOSE . . . 21

TWO-WEEK-PAST . . . 20

US-THREE

VARIOUS-THINGS

(2h)alt.**A-CL**

(2h)alt.**A-CL**"*in a row*"

(2h)alt.**A-CL**"*in rows*"

(2h)alt.**A-CL**"*sweep in a row*" . . . 24